From Hungary with Love

Robin Crichton

Published by Dolman Scott 2012

Copyright© Robin Crichton 2012

All rights reserved. No part of this publication may be reproduced, stored in a retrieval system, or transmitted in any form or by any means, electronic, mechanical, photocopy, recording or otherwise, without prior written permission of the copyright owner. Nor can it be circulated in any form of binding or cover other than that in which it is published and without similar condition including this condition being imposed on a subsequent purchaser.

ISBN 978-1-905553-95-2

Dolman Scott
www.dolmanscott.com

Contents

Introduction

How the Crichtons Came To Scotland in 1088 — 4

The Crichtons of Crichton 1088 - 1454 — 10

The Crichtons of Frendraught   1454 - 1745 — 21

The Crichtons of Dumfries and Bute   Early 12th c - present — 24

The Admirable Crichton 1560 - 1582 — 32

The Crichtons of Ruthven Early 15th c - 1745 — 38

Lesser Crichtons of Ruthven – 16th c to present — 49

The Crichtons of Brunston and Ulster Early 15th c - 1637 and the Earls of Erne   1637 - present — 57

The Crichtons of Newhall 1400 -1646 — 63

Ecclesiastical Catholic Crichtons — 65

Medical Crichtons – The Russian Connection — 66

Other Crichton Families — 67

Conjectural Origins 520 – 1057 — 68

The Children of Adam and Eve — 73

Envoi — 74

The Early Crichtons' Family Tree — 75

Acknowledgements — 76

* * * *

INTRODUCTION

And o'er their grave
The grass may wave,
Their tales are told,
Their ears are cold.

Epitaph in Crichton Kirk yard

No one really knows how the world began or what happens to us, if anything, after we die. But we are all aware of a sense of identity – a curiosity to know where we came from and who our ancestors were. A family is a microcosm of humanity. Knowing our roots provides a sense of security and continuity, which helps to put the world we inherit in perspective. What is interesting is that, in any family, you find the whole spectrum of humanity - rich and poor, powerful and impotent, talented and mundane, lawgivers and lawbreakers. We are what we are and we inherit all of these elements in our genes. An understanding of our personal history is a key to understanding our place in the present.

The first time I went to Hungary, I had been invited to participate in a conference at Veszprem. I arrived by train on a winter's night. There was snow on the ground, it was dark and there was no one at the station to meet me. But with no instructions, a sixth sense instinctively led me up deserted, ill-lit streets to the top of the old mediaeval town. At that time I did not know that Veszprem had been the original capital of Hungary or that it was from here our ancestors had set out a thousand years ago. In retrospect, it was a slightly uncanny experience. So who knows what we inherit in the hidden recesses of our mind and our DNA.

This book summarises the story of the main branches of the Crichton family against the wider background of the politics and lifestyles of the last thousand years. It is about an immigrant family who became the most powerful in the land and gradually sank into obscurity. *"By the turn of the seventeenth century the family of Crichton was in the possession of three Earldoms, several Baronies and of freehold estates in every County between the Forth and Dee from North to South and between the Murray Firth and the Mull of Galloway from east to West."* By the turn of the 19th century there was only *"one nobleman in all Scotland of the name and not more than three county gentleman possessing estates and the name has become a rare one in every part of Scotland"*.

What follows was originally written for my children and grandchildren. The custodian of Crichton Castle, Colin Rintoul, who knew a great deal about the history of the castle but not much about the family, asked to see a copy. As the castle is a place of pilgrimage for Crichtons from all over the world, there was apparently some interest in my typescript so he persuaded me to go into print. Apart from the story of the main branches of the family, I have included my own in the chapter "The Lesser Crichtons of Ruthven". I considered cutting it out for the general publication but on the other hand, in terms of social history, it is a story of the ups and downs of a riches to rags saga of younger sons of younger sons coming through the agricultural and industrial revolutions to finally make good again in the 20th century.

This part is more a family trail than a tree because before parish records began in the 18th century, written records are few and somewhere in the seventeenth century the detailed link of my particular lineage is lost for a couple of generations so there has had to be an element of informed conjecture. But in those days poorer people did not travel far and until the land reforms and the development of industry, subsequent generations remained within a few miles of their forebears

In our case, we broke away from the senior Crichton line in the fifteenth century, when we became the **Crichtons of Ruthven** in the county of Angus – but the Crichton story all started long before that…

HOW THE CRICHTONS CAME

TO SCOTLAND

(Before 1088)

Chance is often underrated in the affairs of men and curiously it was the vagaries of English rather than Scottish politics which first brought our family to Scotland. After the Romans withdrew from Britain, the north and east (Northumberland, Mercia and East Anglia) had been settled by Angles from Denmark. The south (Essex, Sussex, Wessex) was occupied by Saxons from Germany (who absorbed the Jutes in Kent). When Alfred defeated the Danes in 954, England ostensibly became a united kingdom Subsequent kings were elected from the most suitable noble candidates, by a council of wise men, the Witan, but in practice the power still remained largely with the earldoms created from old Anglo Saxon kingdoms. While owing allegiance to the king, they remained semi-autonomous and there was constant warfare and rivalry between the Angle north and the Saxon south.

KNUT (CANUTE). THE SCANDINAVIAN EMPIRE
AND KING STEPHEN OF HUNGARY

A hundred years after King Alfred, his great grandson Edmund Ironside spent his whole reign resisting the Danes, who with the Angle earldoms once again had their eyes on the whole country. Their leader was King Knut (Canute). Edmund Ironside died in 1016 but just before his death he made peace with Knut who succeeded him as King of England, incorporating it with Denmark and Norway into a Scandinavian empire.

Knut ruled England. His sons ruled Norway, Denmark, and the Baltic and Polish coasts. Sweden was loyal, as was Iceland and Greenland from where he sent missionaries to Labrador. He controlled the trade routes down the Elbe into Poland, and down the Dnieper and Don to the Black Sea. His embassy in Kiev was at the centre of the trade route with Constantinople and from the Black Sea he traded up the Danube to Hungary. His fleet united his empire. His trade routes were also important routes for Christian missionaries to penetrate the Slavic territories in Eastern Europe. He made a pilgrimage to Rome and received the Pope's blessing.

As Christianity gained influence in these Slavic states, it brought with it ideas of feudal organisation and western civilisation. This was the time of the Holy Roman Empire and the missionary effort in the East was directed largely from Germany. King Stephen of Hungary was baptised and crowned with a silver crown, given by Pope Sylvestre. As the first Christian Hungarian king, he gave extensive lands to the Benedictines to convert the population.

The church was influential in finding a bride for Stephen who would serve as a papal minder and keep him on the straight and narrow. Princess Gisela from the royal family of Bavaria was chosen as being suitably devout. Shortly afterwards, her brother became the Holy Roman Emperor. She arrived in Hungary with a body of Imperial knights and courtiers. During the four decades of his rule, Stephen organised the formerly tribal territories into royal counties and appointed regional administrators. He invited scholars, priests and craftsmen to Hungary and brutally suppressed any attempts to restore the former clan system and pagan ways. Veszprem, the then capital, became one of the great cultural centres of Europe. Amongst this august body of the royal court, was a nobleman who was destined to become our earliest known ancestor.

EDGAR THE AETHLING AND EDWARD THE CONFESSOR

One of Knut's first acts in 1017 had been to banish Edmund Ironside's son, Edward the Atheling. He dispatched him to Hungary. It was at the utmost extremities of his trade routes but he had significant influence there and it was a place where Edward might perhaps be conveniently assassinated. However, according to the Anglo Saxon Chronicle, contrary to Knut's expectations, Edward *« there grew in favour with good men, as God granted him, and did well become him; so that he obtained the Emperor's cousin in marriage, and by her had a fair offspring. Her name was Agatha.»* Agatha was also cousin to King Stephen's Queen, Gisela.

Knut reigned for twenty years. He proved a good king who brought peace and prosperity. He was followed briefly by his two sons but in 1043 the English crown reverted to Alfred's line with Edward the Confessor, Edward the Atheling's uncle.

Edward the Confessor had a Norman mother and had lived nearly all his early life in Normandy – indeed he was more Norman than English. His reign saw increasing Norman influence in England and ultimately an anti-Norman faction led by Godwin rebelled and in 1052 forced Edward to send most of the Norman incomers back from whence they came. But their stay in England had opened their eyes to a land of opportunity. They had discovered a rich but backward country, ill-organised for war with no cavalry and weakened by constant in-fighting. They had only to wait for Edward's death to take it. But the anti-Norman faction persuaded the King to invite Edward the Atheling to return from Hungary to England. Edward the Confessor who had no children and Edward the Atheling was next in line for the English throne.

Edward the Atheling welcomed the chance to leave Hungary. King Stephen had died in 1038 without a direct heir and since his death the newly founded state had become ridden with struggles for the throne – an unstable situation that would last for years. It was no longer the safe and secure place it had once been.

He arrived in London in 1057 with his wife Agatha, their three children, Margaret, Cristina and Edgar, and a retinue of courtiers. Amongst them were five Hungarian knights one of whom was the original Crichton (except he was not called "Crichton" as family surnames were not in use yet). Although described as Hungarian, he was probably, like the Queen and her sister, of Holy Roman Empire origin and probably like them, from Bavaria. (see later in "Conjectural Origins")

The arrival would not have been welcomed by the Norman faction and Edward the Atheling died in mysterious circumstances almost immediately after landing. Foul play was suspected but never proved.

So the heir to the throne of England and the direct descendant of Alfred the Great was now Edgar, the youngest of the Atheling children. He was still a little boy, not yet in his teens, and viewed as a weakling in both mind and body.

Having been rigorously brought up in the pious court of Veszprem, Edgar, Margaret and Cristina now found themselves in the equally pious but more ceremonious court of London. Margaret and Cristina learned English, French and hand embroidery from a « Mistress of Maidens » and with their Benedictine doctors they read the works of Gregory and Augustine and the Lives of the Saints. They both made up their minds to become nuns.

1066 AND ALL THAT

Perhaps during their first year in the English court, they may have caught sight of Malcolm Canmore, the son of Duncan, King of Scots. At the age of nine, after his father's murder by Macbeth, he had been sent for safety to the English court. Margaret would have been between 10 and 12 years old. He was 23. No one would have imagined that one day they would marry, for within months of their arrival, Malcolm was on his way back to Scotland to be crowned in April 1058. For the next ten years he busied himself trying to extend his frontier south of the river Tweed to the Tees. [In 638 the Angles had occupied South East Scotland when they defeated the Celtic tribe, the Gododdin. For the next three hundred years, the area became part of Northumbria and the land north of the Tweed had only been retaken by Scotland in 1018 so Malcolm's war was simply part of an extended campaign against the Angles].

In January 1066 Edward the Confessor died.

"Handsome, well-spoken and unmartial", a genial talker, a charming lightweight, Edgar the Atheling in spite of his convincing claim to the throne was clearly not the man to deal with the expected Norman invasion. The Witan bypassed him in favour of Harold, the son of Godwin who had so successfully seen the Normans off in 1052. But seeing their opportunity, the Danes invaded Northumberland. Harold marched his army north in ten days and defeated them at Stamford Bridge. This left the south undefended, so it was an ideal opportunity for William the Conqueror to land unopposed and built up his reinforcements. Harold immediately made a forced march south with his baggage train trailing behind. Rather than waiting to muster his forces, he launched into the attack at Hastings. In the ensuing battle, the exhausted and depleted Saxon army was defeated and Harold was slain with an arrow in his eye. Edgar the Atheling was quickly appointed King but was never crowned and it was he who headed the deputation to offer the English crown to William. When William was crowned in Westminster Abbey on Christmas Day 1066, Edgar did homage and received a royal kiss in return.

SCOTLAND

The family of Edgar the Atheling were now dependant on the hospitality of the new Norman king and they continued for a few months to live at the English court. It was clearly an untenable situation and they prepared to leave. Some accounts say that they intended to return to Hungary but were driven north by contrary winds. Others believe that Edgar intended to go north anyway.

To shelter from the storm, their ship put into Wearmouth, in Northumberland, where a huge pall of smoke rose from the burning remains of St Peter's Church. Malcolm Canmore was on one of his raids. He « *granted them peace* » and invited them to stay in his kingdom.

The arrival in Scotland *W.F.Skene*

They sailed north, while he finished his sacking and pillaging. Before long, he returned to welcome them at the rough and simple court in his capital at Dunfermline. He was a ruthless and brutal warrior but he greeted them with chivalrous hospitality. Before long, he was madly in love with Margaret. He was fully eleven years older than her, and already a widower with three sons. The attraction was not mutual. Margaret was determined to become a nun and it took two or three years to convince her that marriage to Malcolm was God's will. Her mother and her brother, no doubt advised by the Crichton and the four other knights, eventually wore her down and persuaded her it was her duty before God. They were all refugees with nowhere else to go. For Malcolm, the marriage made him brother in law to the Saxon heir to the throne - an alliance that strengthened him against the growing threat of the Normans

Margaret and her entourage revolutionised Scotland. She saw it as her God-given duty to improve Malcolm, his friends and his country and bring the Gaelic speaking Celtic Church into line with Rome. She had a continental love of splendour, so the Court had to wear fur and velvet and jewellery. Gold and silver plate was introduced at the royal table. Ornamental hangings appeared on the walls. Manners and ceremonial were made more stately and the king began to appear on special occasions with a royal bodyguard. A room in the palace was set aside for the embroidery of alter cloths and vestments by « *certain women of noble birth* ». All this refinement and magnificence encouraged trade in materials, commodities and ornaments.

The Queen took an active part in affairs of State as well as affairs of the Church. She reformed religious practice through Councils where her husband acted as Gaelic interpreter. She was lavish in her religious endowments and gifts to charity. Malcolm doted on her.

« *He readily obeyed her wishes and prudent counsels in all things. Whatever she refused, he refused also; whatever pleased her, he also loved for love of her. Hence it was that, although he could not read, he would turn over and examine books which she used either for her devotions or her study; and whenever he heard her express especial liking for a particular book, he would look at it with special interest, kissing it, and often taking it into his hands. Sometimes he sent for a worker in precious metals, whom he commanded to ornament that volume with gold and gems, and when the work was finished, the King himself used to carry the book to the queen as a loving proof of his devotion.* »

THE CRICHTONS OF CRICHTON

(11th – 12th century)

Laid waste by war with the Angles of Northumbria, the south east of Scotland was sparsely populated. It needed recolonisation and the development of a feudal infrastructure to govern it. Our Hungarian ancestor was given the lands of Crichton in Midlothian and with it, our surname. *"There came out of Hungary with Queen Margaret wife of Malcolm III five knights as attendants on that Princess who afterwards took the surnames of the lands bestowed on them by King Malcolm - viz. Crichton, Fotringham, Giffort, Melville, Borthwick."* [Chronicles by Holingshead 1557].

The name is of much earlier origin, probably deriving from before the Angle occupation of 638. There is a Celtic word *crioch* meaning boundary or border. This boundary could refer to the western border of the Gododdin, a Brythonic (Old Welsh) speaking tribe who, from the Iron Age, occupied the east coast from the Tyne to the Forth. They had made a treaty with Agricola before the Romans invasion, allowing him to advance north, building Dere St (now the line of the A68) along their tribal border. Another suggestion is that in Welsh *cri* means new. So alternatively perhaps it was just Newtown? Or alternatively it may be a corruption of Car-ric-ton. *Car* may be derived from the roman camp which is close by Crichton Castle (as in Car-lisle) *Ric* could mean rich land i.e. camp on the rich land. When the Angles arrived, they would have added *ton* (town). There is also a Welsh word "cryc" meaning hill from which the village of Crich in Derbyshire is said to derive its name.

The first written reference to a Crichton is in 1128 when **Thurstanus de Creichtoun** was witness to the founding of Holyrood (Halyrood) Abbey. He was probably the grandson of the original immigrant who arrived in 1068. Then in 1240 a **William de Crichton** is described as « dominus de Crichton » (lord of Crichton).

In 1296 **Thomas de Creichtoun** is recorded as one of the hundreds of names in the Ragman Rolls of Edward I of England who, when invited to Scotland to arbitrate between thirteen claimants to the succession, quickly changed the velvet glove of diplomacy for the mail fist of conquest and demanded a mass act of allegiance at Berwick before returning to London with the Stone of Destiny. This was the start of the wars of Independence, led first by William Wallace and then by Robert the Bruce, which would ravage Scotland for the next twenty years before culminating in the Scottish victory at Bannockburn in 1314.

Thomas died around 1300 and had three sons:
- **the eldest son, Nicholas,** died around 1340.
- the youngest son Thomas of Berwick whose son William became Rector of Crichton,
- and the middle son, William, the **1st Laird of Sanquhar.**
    WHICH IS THE BEGINNING OF THE LINE OF CRICHTONS OF DUMFRIES WHO BECAME THE CRICHTON-STUARTS OF BUTE

Nicholas' son **John** was knighted and died sometime before 1358.

He was succeeded by **Sir William the First** who had five sons and died in 1382. This is where the other branches of the family start.

The main line continues through Sir William's first son, **Sir John the Second**.
    THESE ARE THE CRICHTONS OF CRICHTON AND LATER FRENDRAUGHT.

My family stem from **Sir William's second son, Stephen of Cairns.**
    THIS IS THE BEGINNING OF THE LINE OF THE CRICHTONS OF RUTHVEN

The third son becomes Crichton of Bastrop in Annandale, and the fourth and fifth sons, Thomas and Edward were
    THE BEGINNING OF THE CRICHTONS OF BRUNSTON AND LATER OF ULSTER.

Crichton Castle around 1400 as it may have looked,
Courtesy Historic Scotland

The senior line, through **Sir John the Second**, was granted a charter of the barony of Crichton. Before his death on 12th December 1423, it was probably he who built the great tower house, which is the oldest part of the existing ruins at Crichton Castle

His eldest son, **Sir William the Second**, was Sheriff of Edinburgh and Governor of Edinburgh Castle. King James I liked and trusted him and created for him, a new post as Master of the King's Household. In February 1437 the Royal Household was at Perth. They had spent Christmas there, and had stayed on for the Council of Perth where the king was to receive the Papal Legate. As Perth Castle was under repair, the King and Queen were staying at Blackfriars Monastery outside the city walls. It was late in the evening and the royal couple were spending the last hour before retiring with some of their courtiers.

A servant, who had left the room to fetch more wine, caught sight of armed man creeping up the stairs. He managed to shout « Treason » before being killed. Within the room all was confusion. They tore up a plank in the floor, which covered the vault, pushed the king down into it, and replaced the plank. Meanwhile the assassins were at the door.

A young girl had rushed to slam the door shut but the bar was missing so she put her arm through the loops instead. The arm was soon broken and the murderers burst into the room. They quickly discovered the king. He fought desperately but was stabbed to death. The Queen too, was wounded trying to defend him.

No one really knows the reason for the attack – vengeance for some past grudge or an attempt to change the succession. Whatever the reason, all the regicides were rounded up, tried and executed. The following day the king's body with twenty-eight stab wounds was buried in the Monastery. The Papal Legate kissed each of the wounds. But Sir William Crichton has already hurried the Queen and her small son to safety in Edinburgh Castle.

A coronation was hastily arranged at Holyrood and the parliament appointed the kings cousin, the Earl of Douglas as regent. At the coronation, the splendour and arrogance of the Douglass, riding with a retinue of 2000 lances, surpassed even that of the king.

The Douglas guardianship of the realm was however purely nominal. Whoever held the king, held the power. Sir William Crichton, with the king in Edinburgh, and Sir Alexander Livingston who was Governor of Stirling, were rivals and allies. Their machinations alternated from one extreme to the other but were united against the menace of the Douglas's. In 1439 Sir William was made Lord Chancellor.

After a year in Edinburgh Castle, the Queen decided she would be better off in Stirling under the care of Sir Alexander Livingston. She smuggled her son out of Edinburgh Castle in a linen basket. But soon she found she had fallen from the fat into the fire. The Queen felt isolated and alone. Livingston's interest was in the guardianship of her son. She thought a new marriage would strengthen her position. She married Sir James Stewart, the Black Knight of Lorne. But Livingstone had no fear of the Black Knight. He put him in irons and flung him in the dungeon and then arrested the Queen and locked her up in another part of the castle.

The General Council approved his action, gave him custody of the King until he was of age and gave the Queen limited access. Not long afterwards, Sir William Crichton rode over to Stirling and when the young king was out hunting, he recaptured him and took him back to Edinburgh. So, while Livingston had nominal custody of the young king, Crichton regained physical custody. The two men formed an alliance and acting in concert, they turned their attention to the threat of the House of Douglas.

The old Earl had died leaving two sons. They were invited to attend a parliament in Edinburgh and on their arrival, they were received at a state banquet in the Great Hall of Edinburgh Castle. On their way up to Edinburgh, Sir William had also entertained them in his own castle at Crichton, to help allay any fears. When they arrived for the banquet, the Douglas's retinue were excluded. The ten-year-old king was present at the feast with all his Court. Suddenly amid the cheer and merriment, a black boar's head was set on the table in front of the Douglass – the symbol of death. They sprang to their feet and drew their swords but were quickly overpowered. There was a mock trial for treason before the king and they were beheaded on Castle Hill.

Sir William leaving Edinburgh Castle after the siege, flanked by the Red and Black Douglass and King James II on the right.

Courtesy Andrew Spratt

In the civil war that followed, the Chancellor's fortunes fluctuated. In 1440 he was deprived of the Chancellorship and declared an outlaw. He holed up in Edinburgh Castle while the Douglas besieged, stormed and it is said demolished Crichton Castle. But even the might of the Douglass could not snuff out the influence of Sir William.

After nine weeks, a treaty with Livingston and the Douglass was brokered. It would seem that King James II had good memories of his protection under Sir William, which had been far preferable to the cavalier treatment he and his mother had had at Stirling with Sir Alexander Livingston.

In 1448 the King assumed the reins of power and sent Sir William as ambassador to arrange the marriage with Mary of Gueldres. Crichton brought the future Queen of Scots back to be wed in Holyrood and was raised to the peerage as the **first Lord Crichton of Crichton**. The following year, in 1448, he again became Chancellor. The Douglas unsuccessfully attempted to assassinate him but he continued to enjoy the king's favour and confidence and remained at the heart of government until his death in 1454.

One of James first acts, as personal ruler, was to crush the Livingston family root and branch. Their estates were forfeited, and father and sons were executed. Sir William became governor of Stirling Castle in their stead and it was here in 1452 that another Douglas, the eighth Earl was done to death but this time personally at the king's own hand.

William Crichton was an educated man and the first of a line of highly literate noblemen to hold the post of Chancellor. He was described *as « ane of great forsight and singular manhood and ane faithful subject and sicker targe* (sure shield) *in the common weil »*. He was astute and attained eminence from political rather than military talents. He became considerably wealthy and the wider family were also rewarded with lands and titles. In 1450 he was able to lend the King £500, five times more than the contribution of the Earl of Douglas. He substantially extended Crichton Castle employing the best talent available. In the Great Hall there is the mark of John Morrow from Paris who was also Master Mason at Melrose and Paisley Abbeys, Roslin Chapel and Glasgow cathedral.

Crichton Castle mid 15th c
Courtesy Andrew Spratt

The Earl of Douglas was captured and incarcerated in the pit dungeon for failing to pay his respects while passing by.
Courtesy Andrew Spratt

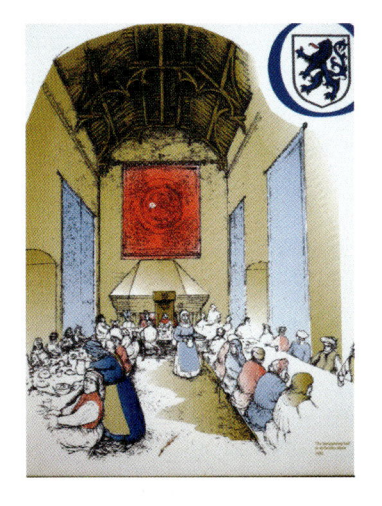

Sir William's Great Hall
Courtesy Historic Scotland

Crichton Castle ruins

Crichton Collegiate Kirk

In 1449 Sir William founded and endowed an ecclesiastical college close to Crichton Castle. It provided for a provost who was supported by all the revenues from the parish and from which he had to support a parish priest and one of the four prebendaries appointed by the Crichtons.

The Bishop of St Andrews appointed another four prebendaries. They each received a share of the church revenues and unlike monks, were allowed to hold private property. Each was given half an acre for a manse and a garden. In addition there were two boy clerks and a sacrist. One of the prebendaries was in charge of the grammar school and another of the singing school. (The well beside the road to the castle is still known as the Scholars Well.) The provost of Crichton was a plum job and, as with the earlier church, was usually held by a member of the family. Indeed in 1427 there was even a supplication to Rome "that Papal dispensation might be granted for George de Crighton to hold the benefice of Crichton even though under age". The new kirk reflected not only the wealth and prestige of the family but also their belief in the efficacy of prayer with an instruction for masses to be offered regularly for the souls of the Crichtons – both living and departed.

Sir William's son **James, the 2nd Lord Crichton,** through marriage, became the 1st Laird of Frendraught in Aberdeenshire. From 1440 to 1453 he was Great Chamberlain. He died in 1469.

Sir James' eldest son, Sir **William, 3rd Lord Crichton** expected to be appointed to high office like his father, the great Chamberlain, and his grandfather, the Lord Chancellor. But it was not to be. Had James III inherited some of the qualities of his parents – his father's soldierly nature that made him so popular and his mother's brains and political acumen, Scotland might have continued to develop rapidly. But James III loved the graces of life rather than its responsibilities and excitements. He had a taste for architecture and craftsmanship. The Scots nobles like Sir William, who by inheritance and position should have been advisors to the king, were ignored by a monarch who preferred sitting indoors listening to the lute and the harp rather than attending affairs of state. His favourites - often men of humble rank – were made political advisors rather than the Scots nobles, like Sir William.

The King's two brothers, the Earl of Albany and the Earl of Mar were both men of the type the Scots were accustomed to recognise as leaders – tall, handsome, and warlike, excelling in knightly accomplishments, great sportsmen, masters of horsemanship and archery. Like the rest of the nobles, they too loathed the King's favourites, whom they regarded as upstarts – men such as Thomas Cochrane the architect and William Rogers, a musician of undoubted talent (to whom the King gave the lands of Traquair – a gift he enjoyed for only nine years).

These men neither had the qualities nor qualifications to take part in the affairs of State and as a result things went seriously wrong, the currency was debased and the economy went into recession.

Sir William's wife, Marion, was very beautiful. The King found her extremely attractive and seduced her   Sir William could do nothing direct. It was a royal perk. In retaliation, Sir William seduced the King's sister Margaret who became pregnant. Marion remained the King's mistress until her death.   Sir William had two children - a girl by Marion and a boy by Margaret.

The hatred between the Kings brothers and the King's favourites was reciprocal. The favourites roused the king's suspicions of his brothers' loyalty and in 1479 they were both accused of treachery and imprisoned. The younger brother, the Earl of Mar, who was only 22 was jailed in Craigmillar Castle where very soon he died. The elder brother, the Duke of Albany was imprisoned in Edinburgh Castle. A rope was smuggled in to him hidden in a barrel of wine and he escaped down the castle rock. He fled first to France, and then in alliance with an army raised by King Edward IV of England, he invaded. War had been on the cards for some time and James had been trying to stave it off with offers of marriage. Only one proposal – a marriage between the Duke of Clarence and James's sister Margaret proved acceptable but this was cancelled at the last moment when news of her affair with Sir William Crichton reached English ears.

King James led an army to meet Albany, but on his march south, he was met by another force of discontented Scots nobles. They offered to join the King providing he surrendered his favourites and pledged himself to revalue his debased coinage. The king refused and the nobles hanged his favourites there and then on the bridge at Lauder (including William Rogers of Traquair).

Albany made peace with the nobles and was made Lieutenant of the Realm. Throughout all this, he and the nobles remained loyal to the King who was now under house arrest in Edinburgh. Albany actually assisted his brother to escape but as time went on, he had ideas of becoming King himself and again conspired with Edward of England. When the news leaked out, he was stripped of his office. There was a battle a Lochmaben with the Crichtons of Crichton on the side of Albany and the Crichtons of Sanquhar on the side of the king. Albany was routed and was forced to flee to France. Crichton went with him

Sir William Crichton was attainted for treason by the Parliament of 1483/84 and was sentenced *to lose life, lands, goods, offices and possessions*. On the death of his wife Marion, Princess Margaret asked her brother the King to allow her to marry him. Sir William clung on to his life but forfeited the lands of Crichton. However, he was allowed to retain all his other estates and with the family moved to Aberdeenshire where the Crichtons of Crichton now became known as the **Crichtons of Frendraught** of which he was the second laird

The relationship between the Crichton family and Crichton the place was at an end. But King James III too was finished. Within a few years the nobles once again took over. They assumed the guardianship of James's son, and James was King in name only. It was civil war. The King was defeated at the Battle of Sauchieburn in Stirlingshire. In his flight, he fell from his horse and became entangled in the harness. Badly wounded he was taken in by a miller. He asked for a priest. The miller's wife ran out into the crowd asking for a priest for the king. A priest came forward, but he was no priest. Instead of the Sacrament he gave four or five strokes of his dagger to the King's heart.

Only 35 years after the founding of Crichton Collegiate Church, construction stopped and the building was never completed, but the choir and transept still serve today as the parish church

The castle was awarded to the family who became the Earls of Bothwell and was the scene of the wedding of Mary Queen of Scots' half brother. The Renaissance wing was built in the early 1580's and James VI was entertained here in 1586 but 15 years later the Earl was forced to flee abroad. The castle gradually fell into ruin and by 1659 was being robbed of masonry for building purposes elsewhere. The castle ruins inspired a painting by J.M.W. Turner circa 1820 and were described in *"Marmion"* by Sir Walter Scott

That Castle rises on the steep
Of the green vale of Tyne;
And far beneath where slow they creep,
From pool to eddy, dark and deep,
Where alders moist and willows weep,
You hear her streams repine.

Crichton Castle circa 1586

The late 16th C. Great Hall

The Renaissance Wing from the Courtyard

THE CRICHTONS OF FRENDRAUGHT

For the next five generations, the Crichtons lived fairly quietly in Aberdeenshire. Sir William's grandson, the **4th laird**, also called William, was certified as an imbecile and was the cause of a skirmish and siege between the family of his guardian George Crichton of Conzie and that of his wife. He died in 1546.

A hundred years later, James, **the 7th laird** became the subject of a famous ballad – *"The Burning of Frendraught"*. On New Year's Day 1630, he got into an argument with William Gordon of Rothiemay. There was a fight. Rothiemay was killed and several people on either side were injured. To avoid any escalation between the families, the Marquis of Huntly, a Gordon, who was friend of both parties, brokered a deal whereby James Crichton paid 50,000 merks to the widow as compensation and the matter was amicably settled. The following September there was more trouble. James Crichton was present during a quarrel between his kinsman Robert Crichton of Condlaw and a James Lesley, which got out of hand and ended with Robert Crichton shooting Lesley in the arm. James Crichton sent him away in disgrace and told him not to darken his door again. A month later, James Crichton was visiting the Earl of Huntly when James Lesley's father arrived with thirty horsemen to demand satisfaction for the wounding of his son. Huntly tried to convince the angry father that it was nothing to do with James Crichton but Lesley continued to demand vengeance. So Huntly gave James Crichton an armed escort to see him home safely, led by his son Viscount Aboyne and the son of William Gordon of Rothiemay (whom he had killed).

At Frendraught the visitors were well entertained and were pressed to stay the night. They were given rooms in a tower, one above the other. But in the early hours of the morning, a fire broke out so suddenly and burnt so fiercely that both men and five of their six retainers were burned alive. Huntly blamed James Crichton and started legal proceedings against him. James Crichton believed it was a plot by James Leslie. He seized Leslie's nephew and took him off to Edinburgh where in spite of his protestations of innocence, he was tried, found guilty and executed. Out for vengeance, the Gordons now repeatedly plundered the lands of Fredraught and for his own safety, James Crichton moved to Edinburgh for a few years where he rented the first floor of Gladstone's Land in the Lawnmarket (now restored by The National Trust). But in the end, the Gordons killed one of his younger sons in 1642.

1642 saw the outbreak of the Civil War. King Charles I needed all the support he could muster. James eldest son, also **James** (born 1629), was ennobled at Nottingham in 1642 and made **1st Viscount of Frendraught** and **Lord Crichton** in recognition of his direct descent from the Lord Chancellor Crichton.

In 1644 when Montrose raised an army in support of the King, the new Viscount joined immediately. When Gordon of Huntly also arrived to join, he was ordered to become reconciled with the Crichton. He refused and so he and his son were incarcerated in Edinburgh Castle. Montrose led a brilliant campaign and by 1645 the Puritan Covenanters were in despair.

But a year later, Montrose met with his first defeat at Philiphaugh. He was still hoping to redeem the king's fortunes in Scotland when he heard that Charles had surrendered to the Scots Covenanter army at Newark in England. A condition of the surrender was that Montrose should disband his army and leave the country. This was in May 1646. Charles was playing off one set of enemies against another, and it was a terrible blow for Montrose.

He went to Norway, deeply disillusioned but with his personal reputation intact. Charles I was executed. His son Prince Charles continued to play his father's game of negotiating with both factions. He encouraged Montrose to cross to Orkney, which he did and started recruiting in Sutherland, well aware that the cause was now almost hopeless. Frendraught was at his side. Before he could raise more than 1200 men, government forces attacked. It was a rout.

Montrose's horse was shot from under him. Already wounded, Frendraught gave him his and remained to be taken prisoner. Montrose was captured and hanged. Realising that he would suffer the same fate, Crichton took his own life. After the restoration, one of Charles first acts was to give a state funeral for Montrose's remains. Prominent in the procession from Holyrood was Crichton's heir the **2nd Viscount of Frendraught.**

The **4th Viscount**, Lewis, continued the Royalist tradition. He supported James VII and II fighting both under John Graham of Claverhouse, Viscount Dundee, and later in Ireland for which he was attainted in 1690. The Viscountcy was forfeited and he was imprisoned in Stirling. He died in 1698.

The line now passed to an uncle George Crichton of Auchingoul, the **5th Lord Crichton.**

The **6th Lord Crichton** supported James VIII, The Old Pretender in the rising of 1715.

The **7th Lord Crichton**, James of Auchingoul raised a regiment for Bonnie Prince Charlie. The Crichtons of Ruthven also served in this regiment and were with the Prince until the final defeat at Culloden. A Kirk Session register at Essil reports that the recruits were very unruly and showed little regard for Crichton's authority. They also appear to have been poorly armed, perhaps because no one was responsible for them. They were not issued any arms until they arrived in Inverness.

Frendraught Castle

After the '45, the line died out but was reclaimed in 1827 by David **Maitland-Makgill-Crichton of Rankeillour**. He was descended from James the first Viscount Crichton's eldest child, Janet. who in 1665 married Sir James Makgill of Rankeillour. The claim was unsuccessful. However having simplified the name to just Crichton, one of his descendants was formally recognised and the family home is now Monzie Castle by Crieff in Perthshire.

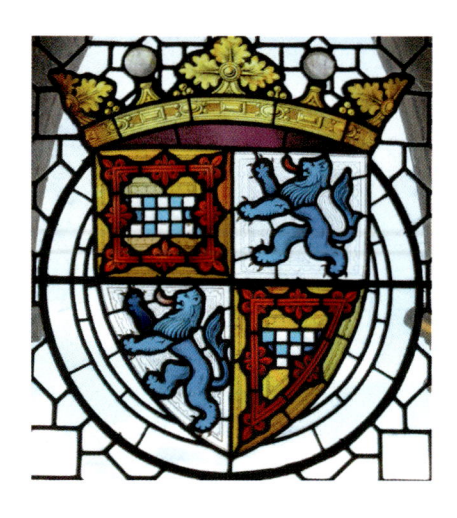

THE CRICHTONS OF SANQUHAR & DUMFRIES
- who became the CRICHTON- STUARTs, Marquesses of BUTE

To recap:
1128 - **Thurstanus de Creichtoun** the first written reference to a Crichton,
1240 - **William de Crichton** is « dominus de Crichton » (laird of Crichton).
1296 - **Thomas de Creichtoun** is recorded in the Ragman Rolls and died around 1300 leaving three sons:
- **his eldest son Nicholas** died around 1340.
- his youngest son Thomas of Berwick had a son William who became Rector of Crichton,
- and his middle son, William, through marrying an heiress, Isabel de Ross acquired the title **the 1st Laird of Sanquhar** in Dumfriesshire.

His grandson Sir Robert Crichton of Sanquhar became High Sheriff of Dumfriesshire in 1464 and later Coroner of Nithsdale.

In 1487 Sir Robert's eldest son, also named Robert, was raised to the peerage as **1st Lord Crichton of Sanquhar** by James III for his assistance in suppressing the Duke of Albany's and the Douglas's rebellion in 1484 (which Lord William Crichton of Crichton had supported). But alas the title appeared to bring nothing but bad luck his heirs.

Sanquhar Castle

Sanquhar Castle is one of Scotland's most neglected ruins. Abandoned in the 17th century, it was acquired in 1894 by John Crichton Stuart, 3rd Marques of Bute who began the work of restoration but when he died in 1900, work ceased and today it is fenced off and in danger of collapse.

It was built by the Crichtons in about 1400. They chose a strong location, with ground falling steeply to the River Nith to the west and the Townfoot Burn to the north. A ditch was cut around the east and south of the site to supplement the natural defences.

The castle, that gradually emerged over the following two hundred years, comprised a rectangular curtain wall, within which were four ranges of buildings. To the north of the main castle was a walled outer courtyard, which would have contained service buildings. At the southwest corner of the castle, was the four-storey keep that contained the Crichtons' private rooms.

William, the third Lord, was murdered around 1552. The Douglas's had their principal seat in Dumfriesshire and were one of the most powerful families in Scotland. Descended from Robert the Bruce, they represented a constant challenge to the crown and for centuries they had been hereditary enemies of the Crichtons who were always loyal to the Stuarts and the Catholic Church. By 1552 the Douglas's were firmly on the side of the Reformation. Mary, Queen of Scots, was still in France and the Regent was the Duke of Chatterhaut. There was a heated argument at Court between Crichton and the Earl of Douglas during the course of which Lord Semple, one of the Douglas retainers pulled a dagger and stabbed Crichton to death.

The sixth Lord Sanquhar was accused on being involved in the murder of a fencing master who had previously blinded him in one eye. He fled to France where he died in disgrace.

William, seventh Lord Crichton of Sanquhar was visited by James VI in 1617. The king would probably have stayed in the four-storied keep. The 7th Lord was created Viscount of Ayr in 1622 and made Earl of Dumfries and Lord Crichton of Sanquhar and Cumnock on the 12th June 1633.

In 1635 he bought the estate of Leifnorris near Cumnock. It consisted of *'a tower, fortress, mansion place, orchard yards and pertinences'*. This now became the new home of the Crichtons

In 1639 he, sold Sanquhar Castle to Sir William Douglas of Drumlanrig, who later became the 1st Duke of Queensberry and built Drumlanrig Castle a few miles away as a much grander residence for his family. But after spending just one night in his new home Sir William returned to Sanquhar where he lived for the rest of his life. After his death the family moved to Drumlanrig and left Sanquhar Castle to begin its slow decline.

The first earl was succeeded by his eldest son, also **William,** who became a privy-councillor to King Charles the Second, and died in 1691.

William, fourth Earl of Dumfries, spent twenty-six years in the army and was aide-de-camp to the earl of Stair, at the battle of Dettingen, 26th June 1743. In 1748, with a view to his retirement as a soldier, he began planning a new house, which would be more befitting to his status. On a site next to Leifnorris he built an elegant new mansion, which he called Dumfries House. *"It is certainly a great undertaking, perhaps more bold than wise, but necessity has no law."* It was designed by Robert Adam and completed in 1759

During the course of construction, his wife died. Their first son had died at the age of ten and the Earl hoped that the new house might attract a new wife into his life to finally produce an heir. In 1762, he married a distant cousin who would seem to have been much younger and a flirt, as shortly after the marriage is recorded that a Colonel Montgomery was *"expelled from the house for being behind the curtain with the new Countess"*. When the earl died six years later, there was still no heir, so the estate passed to a nephew

Dumfries House

The sixth Earl. Patrick McDouall Crichton reluctantly gave up his career in the army to settle at Dumfries House and demolished the old house Leifnorris in 1771. From 1790 to 1802, he was one of the sixteen representatives of the Scottish peerage in the House of Lords. He died at Edinburgh 7th April 1803, in the 77th year of his age. He had two daughters.

The elder daughter, **Lady Elizabeth Penelope Crichton,** born in 1772, married John, Viscount Mount Stuart, who, on his father's death became the 2nd Marquis of Bute. The Stuarts of Bute were illegitimate offspring of the Royal house who had been ennobled in the 17th century. Through the marriage, the Butes inherited the Earldom of Dumfries but only on condition that Crichton was added to the family name

2nd Marquess of Bute

John Crichton-Stuart *(2nd Marques of Bute)*, was a great entrepreneur, and succeeded his grandfather in 1814. He developed coal mining on the family estates in Wales and built Cardiff docks, turning what had been a relatively small agricultural town into a major seaport. He is remembered in the name Butetown, a district of Cardiff. He died in 1848.

3rd Marquess of Bute

Born at Mount Stuart, the family home on the Isle of Bute, John Patrick Crichton-Stuart inherited his title and his vast family estates in Scotland, England and Wales at the age of only six months. On reaching the age of 21 in 1868, **the 3rd Marquis** assumed full control of the family estates, from which he received a gross annual income of some £300,000, which made him the richest man in Britain at the time. One of the first acts of his majority, which shocked many of his contemporaries, was to convert to Roman Catholicism, which he did on 8 December 1868 at a convent in Southwark, London. He then travelled to Rome to be confirmed by Pope Pius IX, before embarking on a world tour.

The 3rd Marquis used his wealth and influence to produce a series of spectacular developments, sponsoring over 60 major building projects by a dozen architects. He is perhaps best known for his restoration of Cardiff Castle and the fairytale reconstruction of Castell Coch, both in Wales. But he also left a lasting impact in Scotland. -the ambitious rebuilding of Falkland Palace, and the restoration of Pluscarden Abbey near Elgin. Late in life, as mentioned earlier, he also started to restore Sanquhar Castle, the ancestral home of the Crichtons of Dumfries

Mount Stuart on the Isle of Bute

John Crichton-Stuart's most striking legacy in Scotland is his rebuilding of Mount Stuart on Bute – possibly the finest neo-Gothic buildings in Europe. Most of the house, in which he was born, burned down on 3 December 1877. As Rector of the University of St Andrews, John Crichton-Stuart also commissioned the building of the Bute Medical Buildings, south of St Mary's Quadrangle, completed in 1899. He also oversaw the restoration of many other university buildings, both in St Andrews and Glasgow. He is remembered as a scholar, historian, archaeologist, romantic, mystic, and one of the greatest patrons of the arts in the Victorian era.

John Crichton-Stuart died in 1900. His estates were divided among his children. The Glamorgan estate of 22,000 acres was divided unequally between John, 4th marquis (1881-1947) and Colum, the youngest son, who received most of the Bute property in the Vale of Glamorgan.

The 4th Marquess

During the **4th Marquis's** lifetime, the Bute family lost a number of their interests in Glamorgan. This began with the sale of urban land in 1909, followed by the sale of the Bute collieries and, in 1923-1924, many of the farms and other freehold properties within the coalfields were also sold. In 1922, the Bute docks and the Cardiff Railway Company were absorbed by the Great Western Railway. In 1926, the remaining Bute property was incorporated under a private family company called Mountjoy Ltd.

In 1938 Mountjoy sold its leasehold interests, and in the same year, mineral reserves were nationalized. So, the major departments of the estate were extinguished before the Second World War.

The 4th Marquis had considerable interests in Tangier. In 1923 it had been declared an international zone and in 1925 a protocol was signed by Great Britain, France and Spain guaranteeing its permanent security. The territory was administered by an international legislative council and Spain was responsible for policing the city. Profiting from the fall of France in 1940, Spain occupied the city until 1945. The El Minzah hotel and the golf club are just two of the monuments to Crichton Stuart initiative.

In 1947, John, **5th marquis** (1907-1956), presented Cardiff Castle and the park to the city of Cardiff. After the evacuation of St Kilda, he bought the islands to preserve their unique wildlife and later gifted them to the National Trust for Scotland.

The 6th Marquis inherited not only estates in Wales, England and Scotland, including six castles, but one of the great collections of European paintings in which he took considerable interest. Works of art from private collections have always circulated throughout the world over a period of time, as various items are sold or otherwise disposed of. Bute approved of this tradition, and was quite comfortable in selling occasional items from his own collection to meet running costs, or to re-invest in new acquisitions or patronage. In the 1980s the National Galleries of Scotland acquired from him the remarkable Saenredam painting of the interior of St Bavo's church, Haarlem, and the National Libraries of Scotland, obtained the fine book of miniatures known as the Murthly Hours.

To offset death duties arising from his inheritance, he had earlier conveyed the centre houses of the north side of Charlotte Square (Nos 5, 6, 7) in Edinburgh to the National Trust for Scotland – one of which is now the official government residence of the First Minister.

The 6th Marquess

As owner of Bute Fabrics, he successfully redirected the focus of the island's main employer towards designer fabrics and contemporary furniture of the First Minister. The fourth Marques had founded a tapestry company the Dovecot Studios in 1912, and John Bute tried valiantly to maintain the financial viability of the company by commissioning and promoting prestigious contemporary designers. It was eventually sold under a different name but several of the weavers created a new Dovecot Studios, and celebrated 100 years of tapestry making in 2012.

He was a strong supporter of the Royal Society of Arts and especially of its 'Art and Architecture' scheme, which commissions new work for new buildings. For twenty-five years, as Chairman, Vice-President and latterly as President, he guided and inspired the National Trust for Scotland, seeing its membership increase five-fold.

His Chairmanship of the Historic Buildings Council of Scotland (1983-88) was equally successful, and he served as Chairman of the Trustees of the National Museums of Scotland from 1985 until his death.

With quiet persistence, he persuaded the Scottish Office to fund a new Museum of Scotland, combining the collections of the former Museum of Antiquities with Scottish material from the Royal Museum of Scotland. After the largest international architectural competition in British history, the foundations were laid in 1993.

To many people John seemed to be shy and retiring. Such an image was misleading. In public life he was always a well-prepared and effective chairman of sometimes unruly committees, but he avoided publicity or grand gestures and disguised the full measure of his influence on public life, even in the domain of heritage and the arts. He refused to take part in the activities of the House of Lords on the grounds that 'the scene' was uncongenial, and was something to which he could not commit himself whole-heartedly. He knew a vast range of people, but he sought some measure of protection in close friends; and also in the renewing power of silence and solitude which enabled him to think, to prepare himself for the unremitting exercise of duty, to study the complexities of large scale issues, to savour and examine the detail of some finished workmanship or design.

Privacy became more precious to him as public duties mounted, and during the onset of cancer from which he died at such a relatively young age. Infectious enthusiasm, however, would always accompany the forced admission of plans for yet another exotic trip to rivers and forests in South America, India or Papua New Guinea; such travels fuelled not only his senses of colour and design, but also enriched his appreciation of the multi-cultural sources of contemporary arts and crafts. Privately John Bute was an extremely gracious host, frequently exploding into infectious laughter or teasing repartee. He always spoke with elegance and wit.

The **7th Marquis** is also known as the noted racing driver Johnny Dumfries.

From the Dumfries line also derive the **Crichtons of Kirkpatrick** and of **Ryehill**, of **Eliock** and of **Cluny**. – the most famous of whom was……..

JAMES CRICHTON, THE ADMIRABLE CRICHTON (1560 -1582)

The Admirable Crichton, James, was born in Eliock House, Sanquhar in Dumfriesshire), and was the son of Robert Crichton, Lord Advocate of Scotland. He attended High School in Perth (or possibly Edinburgh) before entering St Salvator's College at St. Andrews University at the age of ten. James was taught by the celebrated Scottish politician and poet George Buchanan (1506-1582) as well as Hepburn, Robertson and Rutherford. It was apparent from his earliest days that James unusually gifted with a photographic memory. He graduated at fourteen, and was fluent and could discourse in (both prose and verse) in 10 languages (Latin, Greek, Hebrew, Syriac, Spanish, French, Italian, English, Flemish and Scots).

He was an accomplished horseman, fencer, singer, musician, orator and debater. Noted for his good looks as well as his refined social graces, some consider him to have come closest to the ideal of the complete Renaissance man.

He was descended on both sides from the royal family and over the next couple of years, he was chosen for part of the time as companion to the young James VI in Stirling Castle. At the age of 16 he left Scotland, due it is said to a quarrel with his father who became Protestant, while he himself remained Catholic. He travelled to Paris where he presented himself before the professors of the College of Navarre to answer orally in any one of his ten languages whatever question might be put to him in *"any science, liberal art, discipline or faculty, practical or theoretic"*.

From nine in the morning to six o'clock at night, the professors failed to stump him on any question they threw at him, no matter how abstruse, and the next day he won a tilting match at the Louvre, carrying the ring fifteen times on end. His reputation was made. He joined the French Royal Guards (La Garde Ecossaise), and went on to fight in a number of battles in the Wars of Religion.

He had a photographic memory *"Had he listened to a long oration, he could repeat it word for word"*. He could compose Latin verse on any given subject in any meter, and having improvised a poem, could then repeat it backwards from the last word to the first.

Two years later, he headed for Italy but was shipwrecked off Genoa and came ashore completely destitute. His manner, good looks and fluent Italian quickly impressed some of the most eminent magistrates in the republic. In July 1579, he was invited to address the elected prince and the magistrates. If he was a bit of an unknown quantity before this event, he certainly was not afterwards. The text of this oration, which was in Latin, is in the British Museum. (*Oratio J. Critonii Scoti pro Moderatorum Genuensis Reipubl. electione coram Senatu habita*) The theme was that the stable government of Genoa derived from the basic principle of elected princes,

His fame rapidly spread – not just as a scholar but as a heartthrob as well. His *"sweetness of countenance acted like a glance of lightning on the hearts of the spectators and brought the Italian ladies on a sudden to be enamoured of him"*.

A year later he arrived in Venice where his first approach was a poem in Latin, which he addressed to Aldus Manutius, who was grandson to the founder of the Aldine Press and the inventor of italic type. Manutius had probably already heard of Crichton via the grapevine from Genoa. He quickly introduced him to the Venetian intelligentsia – all-powerful people - and on Crichton's 20th birthday there was a meeting of the Council of Ten where it was recorded: *"There has arrived in this city a Scottish youth names James Crichton, who as far as is known, in regard to his social position, is of very noble birth and who has been, moreover clearly proved to be possessed of the most rare and singular attainments by various trials and tests carried out by most learned and scientific men, and particularly by a Latin oration delivered extempore this morning in our College in such wise was he, though not past, or little past the age of twenty, filled the minds of all with astonishment and stupor.*

A thing which, as it is in all points extraordinary and unlike what nature is accustomed to produce, has introduced this Council to make some courteous demonstration in favour of this so marvellous person, who, mainly owing to accidents which have happened to him and to his vicissitudes of fortune is in very great straits; and therefore it is resolved that out of the funds of this Council there shall be handed to the aforesaid Crichton, gentleman of Scotland, one hundred crowns of gold".

There was an epidemic in Venice and Crichton soon fell ill but he recovered and moved to convalesce in Padua where he had a six-hour debate with the professors of the University. When he returned to Venice he issued a challenge to disprove the almost innumerable fallacies of Aristotle, and also the dreams of the professors of learning and he would further reply to their charges. He also agreed to permit freedom of discussion in `all branches of learning concerning those things which are usually openly taught or are accessible only to the wisest of men, and he would reply either by logical and ordinary arguments, or by the secret method of astronomy, or the forms of mathematics, or in poetic or other forms, according to the decision of those taking part in the debate. The event lasted three days and at the end the applause was so great *"that nothing more magnificent had ever been heard by men… .he is never embarrassed by forgetfulness or even the slightest hesitation, as to any things, words, letters, works, and volumes, however numerous, that he has read or seen…"*

Manutius wrote a dedication to Crichton in his commentary of the *Paradoxa de Cicero*. *"It has fallen to the lot of no one, excepting yourself, from the beginning of the human race, to engage, while yet stripling, in the occupations of war, to continue them with zeal and fondness, and connect them like another Brutus, with literature and philosophy….. You have attained before your twenty first year, the knowledge of ten languages, of many dialects, of all sciences, and you have coupled the studies of swordsmanship, of leaping, or riding and of all gymnastic exercises with such alertness of disposition, such humanity, mildness, and easiness of temper that nothing could be more amiable or **admirable**….. "*

In February 1582 Crichton was invited by Gugliemo Gonzaga, the Duke of Mantua to prepare plans for new fortifications. In a short time Crichton became extremely popular. His debates with the local clerics had all the attraction of a theatrical performance. The women liked him because he was young, handsome and witty. And the people just considered him a star.

The Duke and Crichton became good friend friends but Crichton had his enemies - in particular, the Duke's son Vincenzo who was everything that Crichton was not. He resented Crichton's popularity. He was jealous of his intellectual success and also of his success with the ladies. (One account says that Crichton wooed Vincenzo's ex-mistress.) Vincenzo, and his coterie of libertine companions, who were used to being the centre of attention, now found themselves eclipsed.

The prince did not like finding himself in second place and jealousy turned to outright hatred. When speaking of Crichton he always referred to him as a *"Barbarian"* (the Roman term for a non-Italian) and in a letter to the Master of the court in Gonzaga he refers to *"that wretch"*. Crichton voiced his worries but the Duke assured him that no one would dare molest him

The Duke was not in good health and left to recuperate at his countryseat at Gonzaga. Before his departure the Duke forbade his son to have anything to do with a certain Hippolato Lanzone, who he recognized as a bad influence. The Duke instructed the Prince's tutor Donato to see that his wishes were carried out. This was a difficult task for Donato, especially when he went down with a severe bout of dysentery, and sure enough, almost as soon as the Duke disappeared over the horizon, Lanzone appeared at the palace. He was coarse, uncultured and a troublemaker.

The 3rd July 1582 had been a very hot day. In the late evening Crichton went out with his servant to take a breath of fresh air. There are various accounts of what happened but none of them Crichton's version of events. It seem that Crichton crossed the piazza in front of the palace and took a little colonnaded street (now called Via Marconi) heading towards Piazza Purgo. On the way he bumped into the Prince Vincenzo coming in the other direction with Lanzone and possibly two others. They had been out on the town and were looking for trouble. There was a fracas. Crichton killed Lanzone and received a stab wound from the Prince, which severed his vena cava.

The piazza in Mantua

Ducal palace and street in Mantua

He was taken into an apothecary's shop where he died, choked by own blood. (One account says that it was a group of four men who set on Crichton and that he bested all but one with his sword. When the last man removed his mask he revealed himself to be Crichton's pupil, Vincenzo Gonzaga. Tradition holds that, on seeing Vincenzo, Crichton instantly dropped to one knee and presented his sword, hilt first, to his master's son. Vincenzo promptly took the blade and stabbed Crichton through the heart.)

It was a huge scandal and every effort was made to hush it up. Expecting the Duke to arrange a funeral with full honours, Crichton's servants had him temporarily buried in the church of St Simone. Everyone expected a big public funeral but, much to public disgust, it was decided that this would attract too much attention to the Prince's crime. Later on the Prince committed at least one if not two more murders. So the Admirable Crichton still lies in the Church of St Simone with a memorial to *"Giacomo Critonio"….. denominato Admirabile Critonio"*. (James Crichton ….. known as the Admirable Crichton)

The Duke and Crichton became good friend friends but Crichton had his enemies - in particular, the Duke's son Vincenzo who was everything that Crichton was not. He resented Crichton's popularity. He was jealous of his intellectual success and also of his success with the ladies. (One account says that Crichton wooed Vincenzo's ex-mistress.) Vincenzo, and his coterie of libertine companions, who were used to being the centre of attention, now found themselves eclipsed.

The prince did not like finding himself in second place and jealousy turned to outright hatred. When speaking of Crichton he always referred to him as a *"Barbarian"* (the Roman term for a non-Italian) and in a letter to the Master of the court in Gonzaga he refers to *"that wretch"*. Crichton voiced his worries but the Duke assured him that no one would dare molest him

The Duke was not in good health and left to recuperate at his countryseat at Gonzaga. Before his departure the Duke forbade his son to have anything to do with a certain Hippolato Lanzone, who he recognized as a bad influence. The Duke instructed the Prince's tutor Donato to see that his wishes were carried out. This was a difficult task for Donato, especially when he went down with a severe bout of dysentery, and sure enough, almost as soon as the Duke disappeared over the horizon, Lanzone appeared at the palace. He was coarse, uncultured and a troublemaker.

The 3rd July 1582 had been a very hot day. In the late evening Crichton went out with his servant to take a breath of fresh air. There are various accounts of what happened but none of them Crichton's version of events. It seem that Crichton crossed the piazza in front of the palace and took a little colonnaded street (now called Via Marconi) heading towards Piazza Purgo. On the way he bumped into the Prince Vincenzo coming in the other direction with Lanzone and possibly two others. They had been out on the town and were looking for trouble. There was a fracas. Crichton killed Lanzone and received a stab wound from the Prince, which severed his vena cava.

The piazza in Mantua

THE CRICHTONS OF RUTHVEN

15th to 18th centuries

Sir William, the first Lord Crichton's second son, **Stephen Crichton of Cairns** was born in the early 1400s and became Sheriff of Linlithgow. Cairns Castle is a double tower, the remains of which can still be seen near West Cairn Hill in the Pentlands at the south end of Harperrig reservoir. It was the stronghold of the Warden of the Slap who controlled the old road over the hills from West Linton to Baddinsgill across the Cauldstaneslap. Not for nothing was the Slap later known as "The Thieves Road". Border Rievers, Moss Troopers and robbers galloped through the pass on night raids. The family lands were concentrated between Ratho and Linlithgow.

The ruined remains of Cairns Castle

Cairns Castle showing the fireplace and window of the Great Hall and the first floor and vaulted cellar entrances,

Stephen of Cairns had two sons. The eldest, George, became Lord High Admiral of Scotland and Earl of Caithness and occupied Blackness Castle but after one generation his line ceased.

Blackness Castle built by George Crichton in the 1440s

39

THE FIRST LAIRD OF RUTHVEN c.1430-95

Stephen's younger son, **James,** was granted a charter in 1452 by King James II to the lands of Ruthven (pronounced Rivven) in the parish of Brechin, It lies at the western extremity of Angus, bordering on Perthshire. There is a church and a hamlet. It is essentially a farming community, with rolling countryside in a broad strath. It has some of the best farmland in Scotland and one of the best climates. The river Isla runs through the Parish and is about 30-40 feet wide at this point. The arms of the Crichtons of Ruthven are a shield argent with a lion rampant azure on a chief of the last three lozenges of the first. The motto is "Stand Sure".

James became the Lord Provost (Lord Mayor) of Edinburgh in 1476 and remained so probably until 1483. He was Edinburgh's Commissioner to Parliament and is said to have been the first Provost of Edinburgh to receive an allowance of £20 Scots. In 1488, the King appointed him guardian of the money and coin of the realm, and as Warden of the Mint he received a salary of £10 a year.

He was married to Agnes Hepburn (who was probably grand aunt to the Earl of Bothwell who was granted Crichton Castle by King James III after the failure of the Albany rebellion [see Crichtons of Crichton] and whose grandson became the third husband of Mary Queen of Scots).

He lived though the reigns of three kings. James II, III and IV. James III had inherited prosperity and hopeful possibilities, which he dissipated in his eighteen years of futile attempts to rule ending up virtually a prisoner to rival noble factions.

James Crichton's two younger sons Peter and Jasper went in to the Church. There was a daughter Margaret, and his eldest son **Adam** inherited Ruthven as the Second Laird after his father's death sometime between 1494-97,

THE SECOND LAIRD OF RUTHVEN c.1455-1513

Adam was knighted by James IV and was clearly valued as an arbiter in land disputes. He owned several houses in Edinburgh, one of which hosted from time to time The Exchequer of Scotland, which was to an extant itinerant during the 15th century and to which Sir Adam was Chamberlain Depute.

Under James IV Scotland prospered, the arts flourished and there were 25 years of peace. His Queen was Margaret Tudor. When her father Henry VII died he was succeeded by Margaret's brother Henry VIII who refused to deliver the jewels her father had left her and joined the Holy League to crush France. Scotland was France's ally. An English army marched north. James went south to meet them. They met at Flodden on the 9th September 1513. James was no tactician and by the end of the day, he and 5000 Scots were dead. Amongst them were two dozen Earls and barons and many knights including Adam Crichton together with his eldest son and heir James. He left three daughters and another son, John, who was only five years old.

THE THIRD LAIRD c.1508-47

John was still in his minority when, in 1527, he married Janet Fraser of Lovat. They had two sons and three daughters.   In September 1547, the English again invaded Scotland. This time Henry VIII was intent on imposing the marriage of his son Edward VI to Mary Queen of Scots. The armies met at Pinkie Cleugh just south of Musselburgh. The English cannon and archers took a massive toll of Scots and in the rout which followed, 10,000 Scots were massacred mercilessly. Like his father and grandfather, John died in battle against the English,

THE FOURTH LAIRD c.1528-89

John was in his minority and the estate was held in ward. In his early twenties he married Isobel Lindsay and they had two sons and a daughter (Adam, John who became a burgess of Dundee, and Elizabeth).

In the 1550's the Reformation was taking hold in the Mearns and Angus. Dundee was a hotbed of Reformation and inevitable tensions increased between the pro and anti-reformers. The French Queen Regent, Mary of Guise issued a proclamation which threatened death to those who interfered with priests, attempted to disturb traditional services or ate flesh during the Easter of 1559. The proclamation was openly ignored in Angus and the Mearns by many of the lairds and town burgesses.

John Crichton was one of these revolutionaries. In 1560 he was present at the Reformation parliament, which abolished the authority of the Pope in Scotland, forbade priests to say Mass and accepted the new Confession of Faith. Civil War affected the general peace and stability for several years from 1567.

The country was divided into factions of those supporting Mary Queen of Scots and those for her young son who would become James VI. The county of Angus saw its share of division for the next six years or more.

The 4th laird seems to have been in alliance with two leading local supporters of Mary Queen of Scots. After her imprisonment in Loch Leven Castle, her defeat and her subsequent flight to England, Mary's cause was maintained up to 1572 when the King's Party finally gained the upper hand.

On 31st March 1572, Crichton of Ruthven was summoned to appear before the Lords of Council. There had been trouble with the neighbours and blood had been spilled. John's wife died and in the early 1570's, John remarried. In 1574, his new wife was forbidden to leave Edinburgh without the Regent's license and a month later she was placed under house arrest in Linlithgow Palace. John was summoned to appear before the Lords of the Tolbooth in Edinburgh to hear the sentence of her conviction.

John probably died in 1589. He may have been survived by his son Adam but Adam was a "ne'er do weel" and was disinherited. In 1573 there had been a contract of marriage between Adam and Margaret Erskine whose uncle was the Earl of Mar and Regent of Scotland.

They had one son, James, who was born in 1578 and inherited the title from his grandfather. He would hardly have known his father for this is when Adam started to get into trouble,

The Civil War that followed the marriage of Mary Queen of Scots to Bothwell in 1567 had caused divisions between the lairds supporting the Catholic cause and those supporting the Protestant. This lead to the death of the Chancellor of Scotland, Lord Lyon of Glamis by David Lindsay Earl of Crawford - both Angus families. Crawford was put under house arrest in Edinburgh Castle and his family and friends had to raise a bond of £20,000 to secure his release. Adam Crichton was a major contributor and this may have strained his finances. Within a month he attacked Cluny Castle in Fife, which was occupied by a Marion Crichton. There was a dispute over ownership and Adam had a claim. He broke down the door and kidnapped Marion and another Crichton girl. He brought them back to Ruthven where he kept them prisoner for six weeks until Marion signed a deed for Adam to succeed to her lands and agreeing a ransom of 3600 merks. Once released, Marion raised a successful action in court. The contract of succession was deemed unlawful and Adam declared a rebel.

The strife between the Lindsays of Crawford and the Lyons of Glamis continued with several encounters resulting in bloodshed and death. Adam was heavily involved in these troubles. He became estranged from his wife and family and gathered round him a band of desperados. His wife recounts that he had no fear or respect for the King and so set about besieging houses, raising fires, and ravishing women. He plundered their money, documents, goods and gear. He was declared an outlaw and the King commissioned a manhunt. Eventually he was captured and locked up in Ruthven Castle awaiting transport to Dumbarton castle where he would be tried and sentenced. The King was so concerned to make sure he was brought to justice that he wrote to the provost and bailies of Dundee ordering them to place the burgh hagbutters under the command of Captain David Crichton who was to be in charge of the conveyance of the prisoner. But while Captain Crichton was making arrangements in Dundee, the Crawfords arranged a rescue. Fifty armed men appeared at Ruthven, burned down the door and made off with Adam. In the process, shots were fired and several of the Ruthven Crichtons were seriously wounded.

The Earl of Crawford based himself at Dunkeld, flaunting the King's authority. The King was powerless to do much about it and a promise by the Earl of Crawford to ensure that Adam did not trouble his wife or the tenants of Ruthven, secured a stay of prosecution.

But. over the next seven years, Adam carried on much as before. He raided Ruthven at least twice. The first time in 1563 he took twenty horse and thirty cattle from estate tenants along with their household goods and for a while took over their houses. His wife brought the matter to court and the Earl of Crawford was declared a rebel. Three years later he stole another 36 head of his wife's cattle and in 1588, during another raid, he killed James Crichton at the Mill of Ruthven. He was finally brought to trial for both this and an earlier murder. He was found guilty and committed to the Tolbooth in Edinburgh where he would have been executed had it not been for the intervention of his wife's cousin who persuaded the King to commute the sentence to banishment.

Adam probably went to France. The penalty if he returned was execution. But return he did, after a couple of years, and sons of his victims killed him.

THE FIFTH LAIRD c.1576-1621

James would still have been in his minority when Adam, the father he never really knew, was killed. In 1598 he married Margaret Maxwell and they had two sons, James and Alexander.

Scotland was still a fairly lawless place, where disputes were more likely to be settled by physical confrontation and the law only came into play in second place. Gunfights and cattle rustling were a normal part of everyday life.

In 1596, James Crichton had trouble with his neighbours, the Woods. The cause is unknown but it resulted in a shoot-out with "jags and pistolets". While the pistol was relatively short ranged, the hagbut, a gun with a crooked but was more effective over a longer distance. There was bloodshed on both sides. Alexander and Christopher Crichton were shot in the body and the arm "*to the effusion of blude in great quantity*". And three of the opposition were injured - one in the body and the right hand, one in the head and another lost two fingers!

Two years later there was trouble with clan Menzies for rustling four cattle in calf.

James was a supporter of James VI and the Protestant party. In 1600 he was made a burgess of Dundee for his services and in 1607/08 was knighted and went off to join the Court at Westminster. But London and Court life was expensive. In 1610 he took out a loan of 6000 merks. He must have stayed in London a good twelve years for in 1620, he had his portrait painted by Vandyke. The story goes that the King gave Sir James a present of £500, with a recommendation to "creish his boots wi'it". James VI was known for his unsubtle humour! Sir James apparently took offence, returned the money, resigned his office and retired to Ruthven. But after 12 years in London, the damage was done. He had dissipated the family fortune and given a blow to the family estate from which it was never to recover. To pay his debts he started selling off land, but within a year of his return, he was dead,

THE SIXTH LAIRD c.1598 - 1666

James married Isobel Nevay in 1629 and they had a son (also James) and two daughters. He was commissioned by the government to apprehend Jesuits, seminary and Mass priests and other leading Roman Catholics. He was also had up for non-payment of his taxes but by 1634 he was Justice of the Peace for Angus. Other appointments followed: Commissioner for the Loans and Tax (1643), Commissioner to the Convention for Estates and Commissioner to Parliament (1644), also the Commission for War, the Revaluation of Forfarshire (1649) and Commissioner of Cess.

The Civil War broke out. Montrose raised an army for the King. Crichton sided with the burgesses of Dundee and in 1644 was honoured by being made burgess for his active assistance against the Royalists. During his lifetime more land was sold and he was probably about 70 when he died in 1666

THE SEVENTH LAIRD c.1646-1718

James, was not yet twenty-one when his father lay dying. So to avoid the costs of ward of the estate, he hastily married Helen Menzies of Gandtully.

"April 1666. The old laird of Ruthven in Angus, surname Crichton, depairted owt of this life at his dwelling house ther; and his son, young Ruthven, married Grandtully youngest daughter except one, about 4 houris before his fathers death, upon the account the ward of the marriage might not fall"

They had three sons – Thomas, Patrick and William. In Ochterlony's Account of Angus in 1684/85, he describes *"Ruthvine – a little parish belonging altogether to a gentlemen of the name of Creightoune, ane ancient family; a good house, well planted, and lyes pleasantly upon the water of Dean, and a prettie oakwood. He hath an estate equivalent thereto in Nether Glenyla, it and the former lie in Strathmore…."*

It is recorded that there were problems over the state of repair of the manse and the kirk and the payment of the minister's stipend but these seem to have been resolved. In 1700 James arranged a loan of 7000 merks, a considerable sum. After managing the estate for about 30 years he handed over to his eldest son and died in 1718.

THE EIGHTH LAIRD 1667 - 1730

Compared with the long tenure of his father, **Thomas** was laird for only a relatively short time. He was married but died without issue in 1730 so the estate passed to his brother.

THE NINTH AND LAST LAIRD 1675 – 1746

Patrick graduated from University and practiced in Dundee as a surgeon-apothecary. On inheriting the estate from his brother, he had to borrow £800 from the Kirk Session in Airlie. In 1680 he had married Grizel Galloway, daughter of Lord Dunkeld and they had six boys and a girl.

Two of his sons, **Thomas** the eldest and his brother **John** both served in the army of Bonnie Prince Charlie as Lieutenants in Ogilvy's regiment. They joined at Stirling after the Battle of Prestonpans, bringing with them 50 Logiealmond men. At Ruthven *"the minister intimated from the pulpit that, by reason of the present public troubles and confusions, and the distractions and divisions among the people, he was obliged to defer the celebration of the Sacrament of the Supper for this year"*

After the retreat from Derby, these men had dwindled to about 30. To replace them, Crichton had another 40 of Captain Anderson's men under him at Culloden. The two battalions of Ogilvy's regiment numbered about 550 men. They were well equipped and according to some accounts the best disciplined in the Prince's army. They proved their quality in the retreat, facing about several times to hold the Hanoverian cavalry at bay and preventing the Jacobite right wing from being cut to pieces. The day after the battle, on 17th April 1746, the Jacobite army was disbanded. Thomas made his way home and on the 20th July it is recorded in the parish register that *"Thomas Crichton, at the Mill of Ruthven, was rebuked before the congregation for his great sin and scandal, as having been engaged in the late wicked and unnatural rebellion"*.

The brothers fled abroad and by the end of the year the old laird was dead. He was laid to rest wearing a sword as a mark of the family's long tradition of service to the Stuarts. It was the end of the Crichton's of Ruthven. The remaining heirs sold the estate and all the contents of the house were disposed of by public roup. There is a detailed list of what was sold and the price it fetched down to the smallest detail –tables, tablecloths, china, cups, quaichs, dishes, sheets, blankets, pillows, smoothing irons, and an old spinning wheel are among the hundred of items listed. The proceeds of the roup totalled £4311. 3s 11d and the old laird's debts of £482.1s 4d were cleared off.

Two of the younger sons of the last laird went into the china trade. This Quianlong saucer made in 1765-70 was part of a service made either to the order of Patrick Crichton, 1st Officer on the *Earl of Elgin* in 1764, or John Crichton, a private trader in Canton in 1770. It was probably copied from an earlier service, which was part of the sale in 1747 for the design is very similar.

A Dundee merchant, Thomas Ogilvy, bought the estate. The Castle was demolished. All that remains today are the remains of a tower with gun loops. A new house Islay Bank was built nearby. It is a Georgian mansion, and today the estate consists of three large farms.

The only remaining bastion of Ruthven Castle

But while the Crichton lairds were forced to leave, other lesser Crichtons remained. So far in this account I have traced the main lines of the Crichton descendants. I swithered as to whether to include an account of my own line as it is a story of younger sons succeeding younger sons and a gradual decline over the generations in wealth and social standing. But, on reflection, I decided to recount it because there will be many similar stories which are no less part of the overall story.

A LINE OF LESSER SONS

I trace myself back to James the younger brother of the fourth laird of Ruthven, who was born around **1530** and occupied the lands **of East Craig** from 1565 to 1580. I believe I may be descended through his second son (Alexander) and his grandson (Christopher). After this, there is a loss of names for a couple of generations in the first half of the seventeenth century but even without written records, the family remained tied to the land. This was the period after the Union of the crowns when the fifth Laird followed James VI down to London, where he dissipated the family fortunes. And from which the Crichtons of Ruthven never recovered. In 1620 land had to be sold to cover the debts. My family reappears in 1655 with the birth of James Crichton the Elder on the farm of Lenross.

Parish records really only became properly established in 1740-1760. At this time they show five Crichton families in the area, occupying five farms. These farms adjoin each other in a line eastwards from Ruthven before bending down towards Glamis. I presume this represents a gradual geographical expansion as the extended family grew over the generations. As the eldest sons inherited, the younger sons moved on from the farm where they were born to the farm next door.

Movements of my family in Strathmore, Angus 1700 -1800

Before the 18th century the only source of information is mainly land charters, which often go with marriage contracts, but other relatives are often mentioned too. There are rental books for the Strathmore estate and lists of forcible men with allegiance to the Earl.

Lenross, the single story part was occupied from c.1650 -1790

In 1705 **James Crichton the elder** was still living with his son **James the younger**, at Lenross. The farm is on the Strathmore (Glamis) estate, about five miles west of Ruthven. It is a good farm with rich alluvial soil. The building of 1705 could well be incorporated in the present farmhouse where there are still two single storey wings with stone slab roofs which may have belonged to the 17th century building.

Both the James Crichtons at Lenross, father and son, are recorded as "fencible men" – in other words they could be called upon for military duty. At a time when Scotland had no regular army, local landowners were required to conscript their tenants in times of need – a sort of Territorial Militia.

There is a record of the birth of a son Patrick in 1690. This would mean that James the younger would have been born at the latest in say 1673 and his father perhaps 20 years earlier around 1653 putting him right at the upper age limit for call up for military service.

Today, Lenross is a sizeable farm but farming the land in large units was not introduced until the late 18th century. Before that, the land was farmed as Runrig (or in Gaelic "raon ruith"). A rig is a strip of farmland and a run is a series of those strips called "lazy beds". The strips of land were usually worked collectively. The reallocation also meant that each tenant would get their fair share of good and bad land, with no resentment of those with better land. The reallocation would often involve a six or seven year cycle.

So for example at Lenross in 1705 there appear to have been eight other families as well as the Crichtons. It was essentially subsistence agriculture

"*Every cottage family in this parish possessed a house, garden, grass for one cow and one computed acre of good ground. The ground was laboured by the farmer, who also drove out their dung, brought home their corn and fuel, consisting of peat and turf. One half of their acre was in oats, the other in barley. The cottager and his family were subject to the call of the farmer, for what work he might need and were paid according to the rate of the country. With these advantages and their own industry at home, the cottagers in general, lived comfortably according to their station and brought up a numerous and hardy offspring.*"

[Ruthven Statistical Account 1794]

My family appear to have been farmers rather than cottars. At the end of the century they were farming at Overmegvie near Kirriemuir.

Overmegvie (1794/95). The family would have lived a single storey building, part of which can still be seen.

Overmegvie (1794/95)

The old kitchen range in the original kitchen

The farm seen from the house

The eldest son, **Charles,** was born in 1797. He did not succeed to the farm but left to become a soldier. Probably this was motivated by the end of the runrig system and the enclosure of the land into large fields with the planting of shelterbelts and the building of steadings. Perhaps the Crichtons ceased to be tenants because they could not afford the rent of the new enlarged farm and the wages for farm workers who were housed in the bothy and had to be provided with a ration of oatmeal, milk, potatoes and fuel. Some farm rents in this period increased by as much as 500% over 12 years. Certainly by the end of the century all the old Crichton families of the runrig farms of Strathmore had moved away.

"For the most part they have emigrated to the manufacturing towns, and their removal has proved, in many respects, an essential loss to the interests of agriculture, particularly for one article, having rendered country servants and day-labourers very expensive and difficult to be got."

[Ruthven Statistical Account 1794]

The world was opening up. Weaving and flax spinning were important industries. It was becoming a wage economy. Canals carried goods between the east and west coasts. Roads were greatly improved with the invention of tar macadam. There was a boom in shipbuilding. In 1825, Stevenson's 'Rocket' marked the beginning of the railways.

The family moved to Dundee where Charles found employment, first in the shipyards, and then on the construction of the Dundee to Aberdeen railway, which opened in 1850. – *"the port is large and open; the situation of the town is very fine but the town itself is not so"'*

DUNDEE in the early 1800s

A close in the Overgate .c 1900.

A younger son (my great grandfather) **Alexander,** became a master baker and was married in 1857,at the age of 19. The wedding was conducted by the Reverend Gilfillan who achieved immortal fame as the subject of the first poem by William McGonagal whom *Punch* described as "the greatest bad verse writer of his age". McGonagall was moved by divine inspiration. *"A flame seemed to kindle up my entire frame…. It was so strong I imagined that a pen was in my right hand, and a voice crying, "Write! Write!"*

> *Reverend George Gilfillan of Dundee*
> *There is none can you excel;*
> *You have boldly rejected the Confession of Faith,*
> *And defended your cause right well.*
> *The first time I heard him speak*
> *'Twas in the Kinnaird Hall,*
> *Lecturing on the Garibaldi movement,*
> *As loud as he could bawl*

Some years later, the minister's funeral inspired another ode. He recounts that a crowd of thirty thousand people gathered to watch the funeral procession

> *There were about three thousand people in the procession alone*
> *And many were shedding tears and several did moan,*
> *And their bosoms heaved with pain*
> *Because they knew they would never look upon his like again……*

My grandfather, **John Robert**, was Alexander's third son, born in 1870. He remembered that his mother always wore a white mutch (a lace frilled cap). During his life he moved between Scotland and England and he prospered. He was active in the Temperance Movement with a reputation as an entertaining speaker. He stood as a Liberal MP for Newcastle. He became involved in the Thames Embankment Fund, dressing up as a tramp at night to go and befriend the down and outs sleeping under the London bridges.

He championed the establishment of chiropody, which had never been recognized as a profession in its own right and was instrumental in setting up a national association with a professional qualification, not only in Britain but also in Norway and the USA.

My father **Robert Alan** (known as Robin) was born in 1904. He went to Glasgow University to study medicine but he changed in his fourth year to aerodynamics – a field in which there were virtually no opportunities in the early 1920s. He was an amateur poet, photographer, architect, and a car and boat designer, racing his Alvis at Brooklands and his six-meter at Cowes.

Convinced that there was going to be a war, he joined the RNVR when it was formed in 1937, and started giving evening classes at the local polytechnic in navigation and seamanship. He was called up in 1939. After two years on destroyers in the Atlantic as a Lieutenant in charge of ASDIC (anti submarine detection). he was given a six-month shore posting in Gibraltar. He left Plymouth on the 12th August 1941, in the leading ship of a convoy, the SS Aquila. In peacetime it had been a Canary Islands packet boat. On board also were thirty carefully segregated WRENS - "*29 of them as ugly as sin*". By the 19th they were in the Bay of Biscay beyond the range of escorting flying boats. The convoy was bombed for three days by German planes. Then the submarines moved in and at 2am his ship was torpedoed amidships. Father was on the top deck next to the lifeboats but the ship went down in less than two minutes and only the half dozen on deck survived.

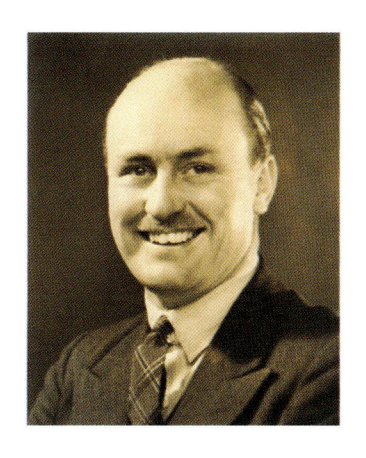

I, **Robin**, was born in 1940 -"a mistake", my mother told me, when my father was on leave! I was sent to school at Sherborne in Dorset, which I hated. I then studied social anthropology at Paris and Edinburgh Universities, doing fieldwork first with American Indians and then in a village in the Taurus Mountains in Turkey. As part of the research, I made my first films.

At Edinburgh, I met and married an archaeology student, Trish Dorrell. Plans for a joint two year study for our anthropological and archaeological PhDs in the Hindu Kush fell through because of military tensions in the area and, by chance, I was offered the opportunity to train under Sir Arthur Elton who had run the Crown Film Unit during the war and was a noted pre-war documentary film-maker.

I built a film studio - Scotland's first – on my land in the Pentlands (once part of the Crichtons of Newhall estate). Because of the near impossibility of breaking into the London centralised duopolies of ITV and BBC, I became a pioneer of Scottish international TV coproduction and made over a hundred films (documentary and drama) before my wife died of cancer in 1998.

I retired, re-married to Flora Maxwell Stuart and moved to live with her at Traquair House in Peeblesshire – the oldest inhabited house in Scotland. I also bought a house in the Pyrénées Orientales in France where we spend part of the year. There I founded the Charles Rennie Mackintosh Society setting up a Trail with reproductions of his paintings in situ, plus three interpretation centres and an ongoing programme of cross cultural exchanges. The French government honoured me as a Chevalier des Arts et des Lettres.

I have three daughters but, after nearly a thousand years, I am the last of my patrilineal line. At the entrance to our family graveyard there is an epitaph, which I wrote for Trish and me but in a way it could apply to all the generations who have preceded me:

>*As we pass on, we pass to you*
>*Some things we learned, the love we knew,*
>*Blessed, we lived beneath this sky*
>*And here, fulfilled, we gladly die*

THE CRICHTONS OF BRUNSTON AND ULSTER – THE EARLS OF ERNE

Close by my old home at Nine Mile Burn in the Pentland Hills, there is a farm, which incorporates the ruins of Brunston Castle. There is a date 1568 and the Crichton lion is still in position over the main door.

The land was granted by David of Penicok to his cousin Sir William Crichton in 1373. (grandfather of the Lord Chancellor). The condition of holding the land was a red rose to be given, if requested, on the ground of Brunston on the Feast of the Nativity of St John the Baptist. His son Sir John gave the estate first to his fourth son Thomas who died without children and then to his fifth son Edward.

Brunston Castle, entrance with the crest, fireplace in the great hall, and exteriors

57

After this, there are five successive Crichton lairds until in 1536, the lands passed to **Alexander Crichton**. At first he was engaged in the service of the Crown on missions to France. He was also in the service of Cardinal Beaton but seems to have quarrelled with him and subsequently joined the English faction. He became a close friend of George Wishart. George Wishart started off as a schoolmaster in Montrose, where the first teaching of the New Testament in Greek in Scottish schools began. But in 1538, he was charged with heresy by the Bishop of Brechin and fled to Switzerland and Germany where he joined the followers of John Calvin (1509-64).

He returned to Corpus Christi College, Cambridge in 1543, and then to Scotland in 1544 as part of a mission sent by the English King Henry VIII to arrange the marriage of his son, later Edward VI to the young Mary, Queen of Scots (1542-87). A powerful Protestant preacher, he was the mentor of John Knox. Cardinal Beaton, Archbishop of Aberdeen put a price in his head and it is certain that Brunston was one of his regular places of refuge while he was in hiding from the Cardinal. Alexander entered into correspondence with Henry VIII's commissioners regarding a possible assassination of the Cardinal, which received an encouraging response. Crichton wanted a promise of both a reward and protection, sanctioned by the English Privy Council, but this was not forthcoming.

In the meantime, Wishart was seized while preaching at Leith by the Earl of Bothwell, taken to Edinburgh Castle and then handed over to Cardinal Beaton who brought him back to St. Andrews. There he was he was tried for heresy, condemned to death and burnt at the stake. On the morning of his execution, the Captain of the Castle invited Wishart to breakfast and slipped him bags of gunpowder to put in his clothing. The executioner fell on his knees before the pyre to beg Wishart's forgiveness, which he gave. When the burning began the gunpowder exploded but did not kill him straight away and his agony was prolonged. Cardinal Beaton watched from his window.

George Wishart's martyrdom was the real trigger, which set the Reformation in train in Scotland. Public reaction was hostile, and by subterfuge, some weeks later, George Wishart's friends gained entry to the Castle. They found Cardinal Beaton in his room, where they killed him and hung his body from the battlements. It is said that afterwards, in the Castle, they formed the first congregation of the Church of Scotland.

At this point it is believed that through Crichton's influence, an English army invaded South East Scotland, laying waste the country almost to the walls of Edinburgh and burning Dalkeith and Musselburgh.

As a result Alexander was attainted for high treason and Brunston was burned to the ground. His lands were given to an Edinburgh burgher James Sym who almost immediately passed them back to Alexander's son John. It was he who built the present ruin in 1568.

They had another estate – Gilberton – which included the other house of Brunston which still exists near Musselburgh, (the lower part of the building dates from the Crichton times). He sold this estate in 1597. His son James and grandson Thomas succeeded him.

Thomas emigrated with his brother **Abraham** to Ireland to find a new life. The house and lands were sold to the Clerks of Penicuik and still remain part of the estate. In the enrolment for shares in the Plantation of Ulster, Thomas Creichtoune received 2000 acres and his brother received a similar amount of land. Thomas's son David is recorded in the Register of Great Seal in 1637. This is probably where the name spelt Creighton starts and suits the phonetic Irish pronunciation "crayton".

Thomas and Abraham built up their holdings in a piecemeal fashion as land became available and in 1655 acquired Crom at Newton Butler in County Fermanagh, an estate of nearly 1600 acres.

Ruins of old Crom Castle.

During the revolution of 1688-89 **Colonel Abraham Creighton** was given command of an Inneskillen Regiment of Foot, at the head of which he fought the battle of Aughrim in 1691.

Crom Castle was of great strategic significance in Inniskillen and in 1689, his son **David,** then only eighteen, successfully defended it against two attacks by a large body of King James VII's army. David was promoted to major general and commanded Lord Charlemont's Regiment during the War of the Spanish Succession. In 1715 he inherited Crom. In 1719 he was appointed Master of the Royal Hospital in Kilmainham.

Perhaps influenced by its architectural splendours, he commissioned plans for a new house at Crom. He died in 1728.

His only surviving son **Abraham Creighton (1703-1772)** inherited the estate and was created Baron Erne of Crom in 1768.

His son **John (1731-1828)** was a member of parliament which no doubt played a part in his elevation to Viscount in 1781 and Earl in 1789. He was one of the original 38 Irish Representative Peers to serve in the Post-Union House of Lords in Westminster in 1801 and in 1804 he became a Privy Councillor.

He does not seem to have been an easy man. Letters from his second wife's family reveal she "*is exhausted, worn out and can no more. He tires her to atoms by his silly difficulties and his endless resolution.*" "*Lord Erne keeps his usual restlessness and discontent and though he requires society more than anybody, is constantly running away from it and yet is without a fund in himself to supply its place.*" The couple lived almost entirely separately and rarely saw each other. On the other hand, good management and perhaps a degree of meanness, allowed him to increase the family estates and leave amply provision for his eldest grandson to build a new Crom Castle.

The first Earl died in 1828. The succession bypassed his son **the 2nd Earl (1765 -1842)** who at the age of 33 had gone mad apparently due to "*cold bathing in a course of mercury, which disordered his head*". He was kept in confinement near London where he lived until he was 80, and the estate passed to the first earl's grandson **John, the third Earl (1802-1885).** It was he who built the present castle.

In 1740 the old castle had been accidentally burned down. It is not clear whether the family had then constructed a new house or whether they moved into rented property nearby but it was not until 1832 that work started on the construction of the present castle. It was designed by Edward Blore, the architect who also completed Nash's design for Buckingham Palace and was known in London as "the cheap architect" because he had put in the lowest tender! It was completed in 1837 but only three years after completion it too burned down and had to be rebuilt. A woman brought up on the estate described it as a place of "*lavish magnificence, of endless goings and comings and doings… a civilisation, a little state, splendid, stirring with life….*"

Crom Castle

The third Earl changed the name back from Creighton to Crichton. He was Lord Lieutenant of County Fermanagh and continued the family tradition as a representative Peer of Ireland in the House of Lords. He was chairman of the Dundalk and Enniskillen Railway and founded a yacht club, which became one of the great British social institutions of its day. He is also remembered as the employer of the hapless Captain Charles Boycott, whose crass mishandling of relations with agricultural workers on the Earl's estate in County Mayo caused a political and public order crisis and provoked the strategy that gave the English language the term *'to boycott'*. Nevertheless the Earl earned a reputation as a progressive and enterprising agriculturist and landlord who sought to improve conditions for his tenants as well as increasing income from the estate.

By the end of the 1850s the farm complex at Crom was probably the best equipped in the country with a silo which was the first recorded example in Ireland. He meticulously checked all accounts submitted to him, and if accused of 'penny-pinching', it did not stand the way of his more than grand financial designs for building' creating and developing. In 1883 the family estates were calculated as 40,365 acres spread across four counties.

The 4th Earl' John Henry' was also Lord Lieutenant and as a Tory peer served as a Lord of the Treasury under Disraeli. He "*earned a reputation of being a clear thinker, a polished speaker, a keen debater*", and a staunch and unswerving Conservative. Like his predecessors he was also highly influential in the Orange Order and when he succeeded to the earldom, he became Grand Master.

The Land Acts appreciably reduced rents payable to landlords and he sold off the large bulk of the estates during the first decade of the 20th century. During the First World War, he was a major in the Royal Horse Guards and was killed at the battle of Mons. His son and heir, also serving in the same regiment, was killed in the same year, so the title passed to the 4th Earl's grandson.

After the First World War, during the **5th Earl's** minority, the estate was run by an agent. Running costs of the house were reduced drastically and the estate was run to at least cover costs and hopefully produce a profit. **The 5th Earl** held minor office under Stanley Baldwin and Neville Chamberlain. Soon after the outbreak of war in 1939, he raised the North Irish Horse but in 1940 was killed near Dunkirk at the age of 32.

The present **sixth Earl,** Henry George, inherited the tile at the age of three. The estate passed once again into the hands of trustees whose immediate problem was to protect Crom from the depredations of first the British and then the American Army, for whom it had been requisitioned. When the Earl came of age in 1958, he experimented with dairy farming and started a toy factory. Neither proved successful and the estate consisting of 1900 acres was acquired by the National Trust. The family retained ownership of the castle, part of which is rented out for events and as holiday accommodation. The earl served in the Royal Irish Horse. He is Lord Lieutenant of County Fermanagh and an accomplished artist. Next in line is his son John, (born in 1971).

Creighton Immigration to America

A hundred years or so after the emigration to Ulster, Creightons started re-emigrating from Ireland to North America. There were Creightons in New York in 1739, in South Carolina in 1772, in Ohio in 1805 and Maryland in 1812. But the main emigration was at the time of the Irish potato famine around 1850, principally to California for the Gold Rush, but also at this time, to New York, New Jersey and Maine.

Demographic records for 1880 show Creightons in Iowa, Kentucky, Maryland, Massachusetts Michigan, Mississippi, New York State and West Virginia. 67% of the emigrants took ship either from Queenstown in Ireland or Liverpool in England. Today the only state in the US without a Creighton family is Nevada. There was of course also emigration to the Antipodes

THE CRICHTONS OF NEWHALL

The Crichton's of Newhall were a minor branch of the family and I include them because I spent most of my life living on land that in their day was part of the Newhall estate at Nine Mile Burn.

Originally Newhall was a Cistercian monastery but King Robert III granted it to Laurence Creichtoune in 1400. A hundred and fifty years later, while Crichton of Brunston, just a mile away, was plotting with the Protestant (English) faction, Alexander Crichton at Newhall was an active supporter of Mary Queen of Scots.

Like neighbouring Brunston, Newhall is in the Pentland Hills, on the highest part of the road from Edinburgh to Carlisle. Agriculturally this is mainly hill and marginal land with large areas of moorland and peat bog. The clue to its real value is in the name of the site on the Newhall estate of the Fortalice of Coaltown. All the geological strata of the Lothian basin rise up to the surface in the Pentlands in fairly thin seams. This includes coal, which was worked from monastic times until quite recently and underground lies a labyrinth of centuries of forgotten tunnels.

The coal is high quality black coal. In Central Europe the smoky brown coal (lignite) was the fuel of the poor, while the rich burned wood. But in Scotland, the reverse was true – the king and the aristocracy burned coal and the poor made do with wood or peat.

In the middle Ages, miners were not free men. The heritable jurisdiction attached to the lands was "of pit and gallows". In other words the laird had power of life and death over his tenants or bondsmen who by law were the absolute property of the laird.

A mine consisted of an airshaft, sunk vertically over the seam, and then a horizontal tunnel, which followed a coal seam. The tunnels were small. You had to crawl to the coalface on your hands and knees.

This system of one-family pits continued well into the nineteenth century. Mechanisation was introduced in the 20th century. The last mine at Brunston closed down in the late 1960's but there is till open cast mining on Harlaw Muir. In the countryside, the foundations of miners cottages can still be seen where whole families lived in a space not much more than six square meters.

The following interview with a 16 year old coal bearer called Margaret Watson on Harlaw Muir, was recorded in 1848:

« I was first taken below to carry coals when I was six years old and I have never been away from the work, except for a few evenings in the summer months, when some of us go to Carlops two miles away to learn reading. Most of us work from 3 a.m. to 4 or 5 p.m. at night. I makes 20 rakes a day and 30 when mother bides at home. What I mean by a rake is to journey from daylight with my wooden «backer» to my coal wall and back with my coal to the daylight when I throw the coals on father's heap and return. I carry on my back never less than one hundredweight. We often have bad air below - had some a short time ago and lost my brother by it. He sunk down and I tried to draw him out, but the air stopped my breath and I was forced to gang. »

In the seventeenth century, there was a boy on the estate who was a cause of constant trouble. His mother was a widow and seemed to have no control over him. The boy was punished again and again for his misdeeds but to little effect. Finally, he was caught stealing cherries in the orchard. The gardener brought him before the 27-year-old laird who sent for the chaplain and instructed him to prepare the boy for death. The gardener, who had apprehended him, was publicly told to then take him to the cherry tree and hang him. But privately he was told to immediately cut him down before he could come to any harm. But, in the event, the gardener delayed slightly too long and the boy died. The mother, believing Crichton had ordered the death, cursed the family, praying that no one of that name might ever have a son to inherit the estate. Although it had not been his intention to have the boy killed, the Crichton was ridden with guilt and went on a pilgrimage to obtain absolution. Some say he went to Rome, others that he did a penance at St Ninian's Cave in Galloway. His sister Mary built a bower on the banks above the Esk where she would go in the evenings to watch for his horse returning over the hill. But the penance was to no avail. He died without a male heir and the estate was sold in 1646.

Mary Crichton's Bower is where my middle daughter Siân was married. As part of the ceremony the minister allayed the curse – for on the land of Newhall, my wife Trish and I had only given birth to three girls. Siân and her twin sister now have sons!

ECCLESIATICAL CRICHTONS

George Crichton of Naughton became bishop of Dunkeld in 1525, having previously been abbot of Holyrood. In 1529, he was Lord Privy Seal, and held the same office in the beginning of 1539. He appears as an extraordinary Lord of Session in the sitting of that court, on November 17, 1533. He died on 24th January 1543-4, having previously transmitted to the pope a resignation of his bishopric in favour of his nephew Robert Crichton. He was not the most devout of bishops. In 1539, in the examination of the vicar of Dollar for heresy, George Crichton said he thanked God that he never knew what the Old and the New Testament were, and that he would know nothing but his breviary and his pontifical!

Robert Crichton, a younger son of Sir Patrick Crichton, Laird of Cranstoun, chose an ecclesiastical career. From 1517 he was Provost of St Giles Collegiate Church in Edinburgh. Additionally, he was Precentor of Dunkeld Cathedral between 1530 and 1534, Under the influence of Mary of Guise, he became Bishop of Dunkeld. Towards the end of the decade, Protestantism took hold in Scotland, and in 1560 the Scots formally broke their ecclesiastical ties with Rome. Crichton, along with the Archbishop of St Andrews, the Bishop of Dunblane, and the Abbot of Kilwinning, were the only prelates to dissent from the Reformation Parliament of 1560. When the Jesuit Nicholas de Gouda visited Scotland in the summer of 1562 to initiate a Counter-Reformation, Crichton was the only cleric to give him an interview. Crichton's solid Catholicism was further revealed four years later when he assisted with the Catholic baptism of the infant Prince James in 1566.

Crichton was a firm supporter of Mary, Queen of Scots, and was one of the castilians who held Edinburgh Castle in her name between 1570 and 1573. For this he was forfeited by Parliament in 1571 and when in 1573 the castle was captured by James Douglas, 4th Earl of Morton, Crichton was imprisoned in Blackness Castle, and three years later transferred to Edinburgh. He was restored to the bishopric of Dunkeld on August 22, 1584, but died in March 1585. He was buried, with the King's permission, in St Giles, in Edinburgh.

Other Crichtons include a Bishop of St Andrews, a Bishop of Linlithgow and several abbots and senior clergymen.

MEDICAL CRICHTONS –

THE RUSSIAN CONNECTION

Sir Alexander Crichton, M.D., F.R.S., &c., son of Alexander Crichton, Esq. of Newington, Midlothian, and grandson of Patrick Crichton, Esq. of Woodhouselee and Newington, was born in Edinburgh in 1763. He was descended from a younger branch of the house of Frendraught and was physician in ordinary to the Emperor of Russia, and physician to the Duke of Cambridge. He was the author of a number of medical books, Knight Grand Cross of the Russian orders of St. Vladimir and St. Anne, and Knight of the Red Eagle of Prussia, second class; he was knighted on his return to England in 1820, was an honorary member of the Academy of Sciences of St. Petersburg, a corresponding member of the Royal Institute of Medicine in Paris, and of the Royal Society of Sciences in Gottingen. He died in 1856.

His nephew, **Sir Archibald William Crichton,** eldest son of Captain Patrick Crichton of the 47th regiment, was born in 1791 and graduated in medecine at Edinburgh. He was thirty years in the Russian service, for twenty-four of which he was physician to the Czar and his family. He served as a Doctor in the Russian army during the Napoleonic War and after the occupation of Paris was Physician in Chief of the Russian hospitals. He was a member of the medical council in Russia and a councillor of state. In 1814 he received the Star of the Legion of Honour from Louis XVII; in 1817 he was knighted; in 1829 he received from Frederick William III of Prussia the Grand Cross of the Red Eagle of Prussia, second class; in 1832, that of St. Stanislaus, first class; in 1834, that of St. Anne, first class; and in 1836, that of St. Vladimir. In 1820 he married a daughter of Dr. Sutthoff, one of the physicians in ordinary to the emperor of Russia. He was a member of the Medico-Chirurgical Academy of St. Petersburg (1853), M.D. of Glasgow, and D.C.L. of Oxford.

Descendants married into a family "of high rank" in St Petersburg and two brothers, William and Alexander, visited Edinburgh in 1892, one in the Russian civil service, the other an officer in the Imperial Guards.

OTHER FAMILIES OF THE NAME

Crichton of Cranston, descended from Frendraught; (David Crichton of Cranston was one of the commissioners nominated by King James the Third, in his treaty of marriage with Princess Margaret, daughter of the King of Denmark).

Crichton of Easthill;

Crichton of Naughton;

Crichton of Cluny;   (there are two Clunys –in Perthshire and in Fife)

Crichton of Invernyty;

Crichton of Lugdon;

Crichton of Crawfordtoun.

* * * * *

THE BLUE LION RAMPANT (520 – 1057)
CONJECTURAL ORIGINS

We know that the first Crichton arrived in Scotland on the ship with Queen Margaret, in 1068, as one of six knights who accompanied her family. Before their arrival in England, a decade earlier in 1057, family history is a matter of conjecture because there was no identifiable family surname. But we know that Margaret was brought up at Castle Reka at Mecseknádasd in South West Hungary in the county of Baranya.

995–1067 HUNGARY

Margaret's mother, Agatha was a kinswoman (probably a cousin or niece) to Gisela, the daughter of Henry II (the Quarrelsome) of Bavaria. In 995 Gisela's father had died and in the same year, she was married to King Stephen. Her brother, also Henry, succeeded his father as Duke of Bavaria and was later crowned King of the Germans in 1002 and became Holy Roman Emperor in 1014.

At the very end of the 9th century, Hungary had been conquered by a confederation of seven nomadic tribes – pagans who migrated from the east under an overlord or Paramount Chief. A hundred years later, in 997 years, Stephen succeeded to the overlordship as 'Grand Prince of the Hungarians' and in 1000 or 1001, he made himself the first King of Hungary. He converted to Christianity. The Catholic Church underpinned political and military power with the moral authority of the Divine Right of Kings and joining the Christian world greatly enhanced trade relations with both the Eastern and Western Christian countries. The Pope helped to arrange Stephen's marriage to Gisela of Bavaria, a princess, reputed for her devotion and dedication to her faith. With her help, Stephen founded a network of Benedictine monasteries and Episcopal sees, meeting resistance to conversion with severe punishments. With God on his side, he introduced the sweeping reforms which would transfer Hungary from a tribal society into a feudal state.

A number of Knights of the Holy Roman Empire, including our family, accompanied Gisela to Hungary, They were put in place to rule a network of newly created counties and to impose the new order. These new counts represented the King's authority and collected taxes, which formed the basis of the national revenue. To impose their authority, they each maintained an armed force of freemen at their stone-built fortified headquarters. During Stephen's reign, Hungary became a preferred route for pilgrims and merchants travelling between Western Europe and the Holy Land or Constantinople. And the country enjoyed a lasting period of peace and prosperity.

Our family would have ruled an extensive territory and we clearly prospered under Stephen. But when he died in 1038, there was no direct heir so the crown passed to his sister's son, Peter. Peter gradually alienated both the clergy and the nobility. When, in 1046 he recognised the suzerainty of the Holy Roman Empire, there was a rebellion and he was deposed. A nephew of King Stephen, Andrew, was invited to return to take the throne. To protect the succession for Peter, Stephen had sent him into exile in Kiev fifteen years earlier. The dowager Queen Gisela returned to Germany, where she finished her days as abbess of a convent in Passau, and many of the nobility of Bavarian nobility left with her. But our family stayed. In the retinue of the new King Andrew, was Edward the Aethling, exiled from England on the accession of Knut first to Sweden and then sent by the King of Sweden to Kiev. At the Hungarian court, he had met and married Agatha, probably Gisela's niece. For the next ten years they lived at Castle Réka in the county of Baranya. Baranya is in the south west of the country, near the Croatian border, so it would seem logical that the Crichtons, who were entrusted with the family's welfare, were well known to her family and were quite probably from the same area. Baranya was one of the earliest Episcopal sees and political "comitatus" (counties) created by King Stephen. Perhaps our family were the first Counts with their seat at Baranyavar Castle?

Under Andrew, relations with the Holy Roman Empire deteriorated and in 1050 Emperor Henry III invaded and there were three years of war. Internally a war of succession was also brewing between Andrew and his brother. In 1054 there was schism between the Eastern Orthodox and Western Catholic Church with Hungary on the dividing line. The days of peace and prosperity were over. By this time our family had been settled in Hungary for a period of about 60 years. The future now looked highly unstable so when, in 1056, Edward the Confessor, who had only recently become aware that his nephew was still alive and living in Hungary, summoned Edward and his family back to England to take up his place at court as heir to the English throne, we went as their escort.

We do not know who else travelled with them to England, but when, a decade later, Margaret and her children continued to Scotland, apart from the Crichton, there were four other knights on the boat with them – Andreas Borthwick, Fotringham, Giffort and Melville.

Borthwick is said to have been Livonian (Latvian). Sweden controlled the river trade route from Riga to Kiev. Did the King of Sweden entrust him with accompanying Edward on his journey to Kiev and acting as his protector during this period of his exile?

Fotringham (Fotheringham) seems to have been Anglo Saxon – a family based in Northamptonshire. Was he the emissary sent by Edward the Confessor to accompany the party on their journey to England?

The other two, **Giffort** (Gifford) and **Melville** were Normans. They must have joined the little group in London, perhaps sent to keep an eye on them by William the Conqueror. But in Scotland, like many other Normans, they switched allegiance and were given lands in the sparsely populated south east of Scotland which had only come under the Scottish crown 50 years earlier and a region where King Malcolm was committed to establishing a feudal infrastructure.

This suggests that Crichton was the only one of the five knights with a similar cultural background to Agatha. He appears to have been her principal protector in Hungary and so perhaps would have been her closest advisor. It is logical that the Borthwicks had had a similar relationship with her husband. Was it coincidence that they were granted lands in Midlothian which marched with each other? Crichton Castle and Borthwick Castle are within half a hour's ride.

BEFORE 995 – BAVARIA

Before we migrated to Hungary, we appear to have been in Bavaria. The Bavarians were a people who seem to have coalesced out of other groups left behind after the Roman withdrawal late in the 5th century. The name "Bavarian" means "Men of Baia" which may indicate Bohemia, the homeland of the Celtic Boii. They first appear in written sources around 520.AD.

In 974, Queen Gisela's father, Duke Henry the Quarrelsome of Bavaria, had taken part in a conspiracy against the Emperor Otto II. The plot failed but ten years later, in 985, he was pardoned. Not all his lands were returned to him. He lost a huge amount of territory, including Austria, which up till then had been part of Bavaria. Did the Crichton's also suffer the same period of exile and dispossession? As vassals it would seem likely.

In any event, around the time of their departure from Bavaria, the Counts of Krajburg acquired land in Upper and Lower Bavaria. It is not recorded from whom. Was it from the Crichtons? Did they sell up and emigrate down the Danube? Were the new lands in Hungary a reward for past loyalty from Henry the Quarrelsome's son, the future Emperor?

At this time, people did not have family names, simply perhaps an appendage of where they came from (e.g. Henry of Bavaria) or a description of appearance or character (e.g the Crookback, the Quarrelsome). Emblems, where they existed, originally related to the seals of territorial holdings rather than lineages (as in the Roman tradition) but gradually the emblems appeared on flags and on shields.

The use of heraldry seems to have originated in the Holy Roman Empire around 800 when Charlemagne adopted the eagle. This became the symbol of imperial power. The lion on the other hand became the symbol of royal sovereignty and particularly in Bavaria.

The coat of arms of Upper Bavaria was and is the "Lion of Sponheim" – not actually a lion but a "panthier" (pronounced as in French) – a beast with the body of a lion and the head of a dragon (*argent, a panther rampant azure, armed Or and langued gules*). Nowadays, the fire-spitting panthier is the Coat of Arms of the city of Ingolstadt in Upper Bavaria. It lies a little to the north of Munich, on the banks of the Danube.

Arms of Ingolstadt and Upper Bavaria

The original Crichton arms are a blue lion with a crest of a green fire-spitting dragon. Is this derived from the original dragon/lion combination now in the arms of Upper Bavaria? The lion is the king of beasts and was the symbol of royal sovereignty and particularly in Bavaria.

If there was ever any symbolism in the arms it is not recorded. However it has been suggested that the colour blue (*azure*) symbolises strength, courage, and a quality of politic in council – in other words a foe to fear. The white (*argent*) ground signifies strength, sincerity, peace and purity reinforced by the original motto of "God Send Grace" or of my branch of the family "Stand Sure". On the crest the green dragon represents keen sight and symbolises a valiant defender of treasure, Green (*vert*) is the colour of loyalty and red (*gules*) signifies magnanimity and military strength

Alternatively, the blue lion, which was incorporated into the arms of Bavaria in 1835 (Ludwig I), is on the arms of Valdenz, originally a county on the Moselle, which belonged to Bavaria from 1777 to 1797. Around about 500BC, the Valdenz valley was settled by a people of mixed Germanic and Celtic stock called the Traveri, who from about 50BC to 500AD became part of the Roman Empire

The arms of the ancestors in Bavaria would have been territorial and would have presumably been passed on with the lands, which were sold. In tribal Hungary, at this time, there were no arms. Did the immigrant family design new arms for their new lands? Did they reutilise the symbols of the blue lion and the dragon and then, half a century later, bring those emblems with them to Scotland? Is the blue lion a clue to the Dark Age origins of the family that became the Crichtons of Scotland? It is of course highly conjectural but with the lack of any written records it seems a possible hypothesis? The three lozenges on the arms of Ruthven indicate that it is the third branch of the family, after the Crichtons of Crichton and Frendraught, and the Crichtons of Dumfries. (the Crichtons of Brunstane and Erne were the fourth)

Arms of Bavaria    *Arms of Crichton of Ruthven*    *Arms of Valdenz*

THE CHILDREN OF ADAM AND EVE

To try and shed some light on this hypothesis, I had my DNA analysed. The Y chromosome is only passed down through the male line so should apply to all male Crichtons. I discovered that my DNA markers are M269+S21+S116.

Modern humans first appear in the fossil record in Africa about 195,000 years ago. Around 60,000 years ago, people began to trek north and east to the Horn of Africa and across the narrows of the Red Sea – nomadic groups of hunter-gatherers. But around 8500BC in the Fertile Crescent which stretched from Iraq through Syria to the Levant, these early people began to grow crops. They planted orchards and gardens and wild grasses began to be cultivated as cereals. This more settled existence led to land ownership and a rapid increase in population.

My M269 marker defines me as 'Anatolian', which means that, during the Ice Age, my ancestors survived in what is now Western Turkey. After the weather began to warm, around 11000 BC the majority of the tribe remained in Anatolia but a small group migrated north crossing the Bosphorus to slowly move up through the Balkans to cross the Alps into an empty and unknown landscape. Two or three millennia later they would have begun to farm, domesticating animals and growing crops. Otzi, the hunter found preserved in an Alpine glacier is Europe's earliest mummy. He lived from around 3300 to 3255.BC and was not much smaller than us. He was 5'5'" high and weighed 10stone 9 lbs.

My S21 and S116 markers appear to emanate from the western and eastern Rhine river basins so this seems to confirm our presence in the area around Upper Bavaria, which by the 6th century BC had become the heartland of the early Celtic culture. By the time of Christ it had been absorbed into the Roman Empire and interestingly Latin writers note an ethnic connection with other Celtic tribes (Liburnians) further south in Austria, Slovenia and on the Dalmatian Coast, the route of our earlier migration.

Today our DNA marker is carried by 17% of the Anatolian population. In Scotland it is only 2% (with the main percentage in the South West and South East). In Germany and Central Europe it is 5%.

If some of the of the Dark Age history is hypothetical, the DNA indisputably take us back to Y chromosome Adam – the first Homus Erectus in the Garden of sub-Saharan Africa. A family history cannot extend further than that!

ENVOIE

From the one original ancestor who arrived by ship with the future Queen of Scotland in 1068, the family of Crichton rose to become one of the most powerful in Scotland. Our decline was largely due to loyalty to king and religion and a failure to anticipate political change.

From at least the seventeenth century, there was an increasing trickle of emigration as different families chose to seek a better life abroad.

The name with its CH in the middle, can be confusing to pronounce and over the centuries, there have been many variations in the spelling. The English often pronounce it Critchton. The Irish say Crayton. In France, I am pronounced as Creeshtonne but there also appear to be Critons. In German, it is pronounced Creechtone (suggesting a "creaky sound"!) and sometimes written as Krichton or Krechton. There are Creyghton's, Creijghtons or Kreyghtons in the Netherlands and I believe Critonskis in Russia. In Scandinavia they seem to have remained as Crichtons.

And there are many other spellings of the name: - Crecon (in 1136), Cristoun, Crichtoun, Crechtune, Creychtoun, Criton, Chrichton, Criten, Cryton, Chriton, Crichten, Creighton, Creyghton, Creaton, Craighton, Cretan, Craton, Creeton, Crichten, Chreichton, Creichtone, Creychton, Creychtoun, Creychtoune, Craton, Crayton, Kreitton or Kreittoun, Kregton, and Kruchten,

But in the annals of time, however you write or pronounce our name, we are all one international family tree, the people of the blue lion, who two and a half thousand years ago were probably rooted somewhere in Central Europe but whose branches are now spread throughout the world.

THE EARLY CRICHTONS

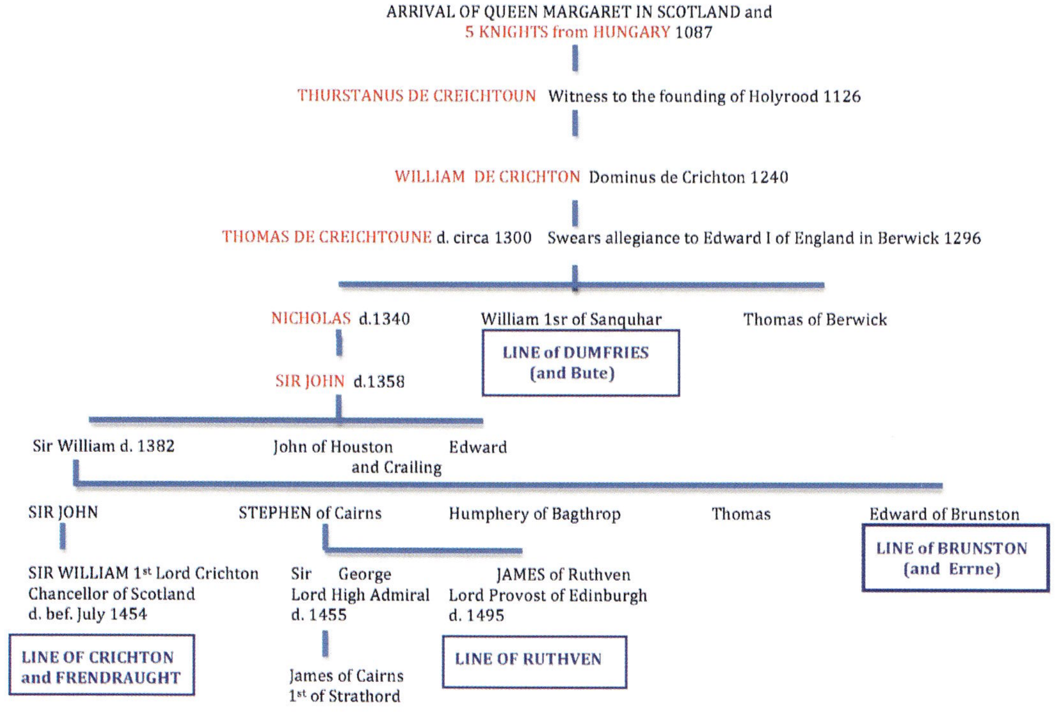

ARRIVAL OF QUEEN MARGARET IN SCOTLAND and
5 KNIGHTS from HUNGARY 1087

THURSTANUS DE CREICHTOUN Witness to the foundling of Holyrood 1126

WILLIAM DE CRICHTON Dominus de Crichton 1240

THOMAS DE CREICHTOUNE d. circa 1300 Swears allegiance to Edward I of England in Berwick 1296

- William 1sr of Sanquhar — Thomas of Berwick
  - **LINE of DUMFRIES (and Bute)**
- NICHOLAS d.1340 — John of Houston and Crailing — Edward
- SIR JOHN d.1358
  - Sir William d. 1382
  - SIR JOHN
  - SIR WILLIAM 1st Lord Crichton Chancellor of Scotland d. bef. July 1454
    - **LINE OF CRICHTON and FRENDRAUGHT**
  - STEPHEN of Cairns
    - Sir George Lord High Admiral d. 1455
    - James of Cairns 1st of Strathord
- Humphery of Bagthrop — Thomas
  - JAMES of Ruthven Lord Provost of Edinburgh d. 1495
  - **LINE OF RUTHVEN**
- Edward of Brunston
  - **LINE of BRUNSTON (and Errne)**

75

ACKNOWLEDGEMENTS

I would like to thank:

My daughter Siân who bullied me into researching and writing down what I knew for my grandchildren Nathalie, Kieren, Calum and Flynn.

My daughters Miglet and Louise for their help and corrections.

Colin Rintoul, guardian of Crichton Castle, for prompting me to publish the results.

The Marquis of Bute, the Earl of Erne and Gordon Morison of Frendraught for their help with illustrations and corrections to the text.

Historic Scotland and Andrew Spratt for the right to use their illustrations.

And Flora Crichton who tolerates my long absences in the arms of my computer.

Tourist Note

Crichton Castle (Historic Scotland), Dumfries House (National Trust for Scotland), and Mount Stuart (Marquess of Bute) are all open to the public.

Crichton Collegiate Church is a working parish church.

Sanquhar Castle is also open to visit but dangerous to enter.

Frendraught, Monzie, Newhall and Brunston are all private property.